371 Harmonized Chorales

and

69 Chorale Melodies

with figured bass

by

JOHANN SEBASTIAN BACH

This publication of the 371 has been entirely

revised, corrected, edited, and annotated

by

ALBERT RIEMENSCHNEIDER

Ed. 1679

G. SCHIRMER, Inc.

DISTRIBUTED BY

7777 W. BLUEMOUND RD. P.O. BOX 13819 MILWAUKEE, WI 53213

CONTENTS

	PAGE
GENERAL PREFACE TO THE CHORALES.	v
INDEX OF THE CHORALES ACCORDING TO PAGE.	xi
MUSIC:	
The 371 Chorales	1
The 69 Chorale Melodies	91
COMMENTARY:	
(on the 371)	
The 371 Chorale Harmonizations	108
Index of the 371 Chorales According to Number.	110
Abbreviations Used in the Ensuing Notes.	112
Notes on the 371 Chorales	113
(on the 69)	
The 69 Chorale Melodies with Figured Bass.	163
Index of the 69 Chorale Melodies According to Number	164

THE 371 CHORALES
AND THE 69 CHORALE MELODIES

GENERAL PREFACE TO THE CHORALES

PROBABLY NO MUSIC publication in existence today has enjoyed so long a period of continued popularity and usefulness as the present one, the 371 four-voiced chorales (*371 vierstimmige Choralgesänge*) harmonized by Johann Sebastian Bach.

In the field of harmony, this collection has guided students and artists alike for over 150 years. During that time it has undergone only slight alteration. The most extensive changes were those made in 1831 for the so-called third printing (*dritte Auflage*). At that time the format was altered and the upper staff throughout was changed from the soprano C-clef to the more popular G-clef. In the original edition, moreover, two chorales had been given the same number, 283; in the 1831 edition, the chorales beginning with 283b were renumbered, thus making a total of 371 instead of 370. Aside from these and a few minor changes, the publication has carried on its extremely useful career without interruption and without other alteration. Further on in this preface a short history of it will be given, along with a history of other important editions of the chorales.

The Chorale in the Works of J. S. Bach

Although the chorales by J. S. Bach were among the first groups of his compositions to be collected after his death, many false impressions still prevail regarding them, owing largely to the fact that the majority of those to whom the editing and publishing of these important works were entrusted were themselves either uninformed or indifferent about the salient facts concerning these gems of music literature. Some clarification of essentials will help towards a better understanding.

Let us begin by saying that the melodies of these chorales were in only a few instances created by J. S. Bach. In the large majority of cases the melodies are those from the vast number that were in current use by the Lutheran church. These melodies were derived from secular (folksong) and Gregorian sources, as well as developed in the church itself, and had the advantage of an intense popular appreciation.

The manner and extent to which Bach made use of these melodies in his work has no counterpart in music history. He is generally credited with having written approximately three hundred sacred cantatas. A glance over a catalogue of the names of the two hundred cantatas that survive impresses one with the frequent coincidence of the titles of these cantatas with the names of the chorales then in general use. In the majority of cases Bach's cantatas end with a chorale; and, in a large number of them, each movement of the cantata presents some treatment of the chorale melody. Excellent examples of this type are Cantatas No. 4, "Christ lag in Todesbanden", and No. 80, "Ein feste Burg". It is not an exaggeration to say that Bach based his compositions for the church upon the chorale. The manner in which the chorale has found its application in these masterpieces is one of the evidences of the genius of the great master.

In addition to using the chorale as the basis of his vocal compositions, Bach also used a limited number of chorales as single entities. In the little *Notenbuch* for his second wife, Anna Magdalena Bach, are found several detached examples of chorales and chorale harmonizations; and in a manuscript written by Bach's pupil, Johann Ludwig Krebs, are found several more. There exist also three separate "Wedding Chorales" with instrumental accompaniment. In a hymnbook compiled by Georg Christian Schemelli are found a considerable number of melodies supplied with figured basses by J. S. Bach. Designed for domestic devotional services or for congregational use, they were not supplied with the complete harmonizations, thus leaving the organist free to improvise the accompaniment according to the demands of each verse as needed. This was in accordance with Bach's expressed admonishment to his pupils to *play* the *words* of the chorale in accompanying the singing of the congregation. From the printed list of the estate of Carl Philipp Emanuel Bach, we learn that J. S. Bach made a harmonized version of 88 chorales of this type for his own personal use. There is a possibility that some of these may have found their way into the present collection of 371 chorales. More will be said about this later.

69 Melodies with Figured Bass from G. C. Schemelli's Gesang-Buch

The 69 chorale melodies with figured bass that were published by C. F. Becker as an addendum to the 371 Chorales in 1832 have assumed a place of importance in music literature since, during the last several years, they have been issued by various publishers under the name of *Geistliche Lieder und Arien* (Spiritual Songs and Arias). They are being used increasingly by *Lieder* singers for concert performances and by church singers for the church services.

These 69 chorale melodies with figured bass are derived from Georg Christian Schemelli's *Musikalisches Gesang-Buch*, a book of 954 hymns published by B. C. Breitkopf in 1736. Of these 69 melodies, Johannes Zahn in his monumental work *Die Melodien der deutschen evangelischen Kirchenlieder* attributes 21 to Bach and the rest to other composers. He attributes the following numbers of the 69 to Bach himself since they appeared in Schemelli's *Gesang-Buch* for the first time: 7, 10, 11, 14, 19, 21, 30, 31, 42, 44, 46, 47, 52, 53, 56, 59, 62, 64, 66, 67, and 68. Of these, the only one that has Bach's signature is No. 44. Max Seiffert, in his edition published in 1924 by Bärenreiter, agrees with this classification. Charles Sanford Terry, in his *J. S. Bach's Original Hymn Tunes for Congregational Use*, published by the Oxford University Press in 1922, disagrees in part: he claims that Nos. 10, 11, 21, 52, and 66 of the 69 do not show the characteristics of Bach, and he consequently excludes them from his collection.

Those who are interested in comparing their own realization of the basses with some harmonized by Bach will find No. 18 of the 69 completely harmonized as No. 220 of the 371; similarly, No. 22 as No. 172, No. 26 as No. 206, No. 36 as No. 234, No. 53 as No. 244, No. 55 as No. 193, No. 63 as No. 346, and No. 65 as No. 213. In one or two of these pairs slight differences occur, but they offer many interesting points of comparison.

In realizing the basses, one will find at times that the bass lies so near the soprano that not

even a simple triad can be conveniently placed between them. Two things must be taken into consideration at this point: first, that the melodies were probably designed to be sung as solos or in unison, with the accompanist filling out the harmonies at the instrument, and, second, that the *continuo* or instrumental bass was usually played an octave lower than the vocal bass. This gave an opportunity for the tenor to cross under the bass, as it frequently does in harmonizations made by Bach himself.

Bach's contribution to the melodies of other composers in Schemelli's *Gesang-Buch* consisted, in addition to very slight other changes, in adding a virile bass part and the figures for the indicated harmonies. One of the strongest features of Bach's compositions is, no doubt, the progressions of his basses. This makes the contribution a notable one.

The "69" in the present published form may be used for a number of purposes. They can be used by harmony students to realize at the piano the harmonies from the given figures and the basses. By comparing them with the various editions of the published sets of spiritual songs, students of composition can find excellent examples showing how to work out simple accompaniments to a melody. The "69" have also been arranged for four-part chorus by Franz Wüllner, in the Neue Bachgesellschaft edition (1901): this presents still another basis of comparison for the student of harmony and composition. As a corollary to the 371 harmonized chorales they form a splendid addition to these standard works.

Other Forms of Chorales

Another form of harmonized chorale is found in the organ works. A few simple harmonizations exist there that may have been derived from the 88 mentioned above. There are four extended sets of chorale variations for the organ, the last of which, "Vom Himmel hoch", a masterwork in canonic form, is the only one not preceded by a simple harmonization. The real organ chorale, as found in the *Little Organ Book*, is written in the form of the vocal chorale but in the more elaborate idiom of the organ instead of the voice. Beyond these there exist for the organ numerous chorale preludes and fantasies of many types, from very short compositions to forms of very extended and complex structure. Approximately half of Bach's organ compositions are based upon the chorale.

By far the most frequent application of the chorale is found in works written by Bach specifically for the church. These include his cantatas, motets, passions, oratorios, and other works. The manner of application is so varied as to defy description in a limited preface such as this.

First, there are the simple, harmonized chorales in motet style. In this form the instruments used for the performance of the cantata duplicate the voice parts, only very exceptionally adding a note here and there to fill in the harmony or to supply passing notes. As a rule the pedal bass of the organ or the contrabass, or both, played the vocal bass one octave lower. Sometimes this led to a slight elaboration of the instrumental bass and gave rise to errors in the publication of the chorales by confusing the vocal bass and the *continuo* part.

It might be well to state here that Bach never intended his chorale harmonizations to be sung *a cappella* and that, in all of those derived from existing works, an orchestra was assigned to assist. The motet type of chorale was the simplest form that appeared in his larger compositions.

Another simple form of application was the introduction of a chorale melody by some instrument or voice part into an otherwise complete ensemble. A splendid example of this is found in the trio for women's voices "Suscepit Israel" from the Magnificat, where the oboes intone the Tonus Peregrinus, which was in prevalent use as the German Magnificat. The use of the chant in the "Confiteor" Chorus of the great Mass in B minor is another unusual example of an appropriate use of such a melody. These examples are quoted since works such as the Magnificat and the Masses would ordinarily preclude the use of chorales. Perhaps the most extended application of this kind is found in the opening chorus of the St. Matthew Passion.

The use of the harmonized chorale grouped in stanza sections, in motet style, with interludes, is quite frequent. These interludes may assume the form of orchestral interludes or, at times,

only short passages consisting of recitative or solo sentences.

Harmonized chorales used as an integral part with *obbligato* instrumental parts are very common. These *obbligati* instruments vary from one instrument such as a flute, a violin, an oboe, or a horn to a complete set of instruments as used by Bach.

Beyond the scope of the solidly harmonized chorales are the great chorale fantasies of the cantatas and other works. A good example is the opening chorus of Cantata No. 80, "Ein feste Burg". Here each verse-line of the melody is in turn used as the basis of a separate exposition. While these different sections are presented, the complete chorale melody in canonic imitation appears with marvellous ingenuity above and below the composition proper. These various uses of the chorale melody show how highly they were valued by Bach.

With the exception of the Schemelli numbers and a very few others, the harmonized chorales of J. S. Bach are taken from his larger works. Those larger works that are still in existence contain approximately only one-half of the known chorales. It is a fairly certain deduction that the larger number of the other half were part of those compositions that are now known to have been lost, among which were about a hundred cantatas. It is thus by a fortunate circumstance that we have preserved for us the chorale harmonizations of these works, because someone had made a collection of the chorales while these works were still in existence.

For the chorales that are contained in those works still existing, we are fortunate in being able to find a record of the details of performance as desired by Bach. The instrumentation and surroundings of the chorale are known, as well as the actual words of the chorale that were selected by Bach. It is now well known that Bach's method of setting a chorale was directly influenced by the words used. This has been investigated in the minutest detail by Schering, Schweitzer, and especially by Pirro in his *L'Esthétique de J. S. Bach.* In those chorales for which we know the original words, a close study of the relation of music and words is most instructive. A specialized continuation of Pirro's searching investigations applied specifically to chorale harmonizations might make it possible to restore the original words to those chorales for which the text has been lost. This would be a wonderful help in grasping the full significance of these unusual and marvellous harmonizations. The fact remains that the results cannot be explained from a purely musical standpoint, and only the association of the text makes it possible to solve some of the strange chords and progressions.

Perhaps the outstanding example of such a misunderstanding is the work published by Abt Vogler in 1810, for which Carl Maria von Weber wrote the preface. In this work Vogler set up twelve chorales harmonized by Bach and, because he did not know the words that led to some of the harmonic results, criticized them and placed twelve harmonizations of his own opposite those of Bach in order to show how they should have been written. Had he known the words of the chorales, he would never have committed this ludicrous blunder. The words are, accordingly, of the utmost importance in the study of these chorales. They offer opportunities to study the tone-painting and aesthetics that permeate these chorale harmonizations almost as much as his larger chorale works. Erk, in the second volume of the Peters Edition (1865) attempted to supply the missing texts to numerous chorales but did not have the advantage offered by the modern research of Pirro.

For a complete understanding of these chorales the student should do much more than study merely the harmonizations, interesting as they are. An important aspect of each chorale-harmonization is its place in the larger work of which it forms a part, and also its relation to the whole composition. The student's problem as he first encounters one of the harmonizations is somewhat like that of a scientist who has before him one important fossil part of a prehistoric animal. This relationship of chorale to the whole work is necessary in order to learn what the composer meant to do with the chorale.

A short history of the chief publications of the chorales will show how the lack of attention to these details has led to the present chaos in the understanding of the chorales.

History of the Publication of the Bach Chorales

In 1764 the firm "Breitkopf und Sohn" announced for sale manuscript copies of 150 chorale harmonizations by J. S. Bach, and also manuscript copies of 240 chorale melodies with figured basses. These are the first known references to the sale of a group of collected chorales by J. S. Bach.

In 1765 the first publication of 100 of these chorales was issued by F. W. Birnstiel at Berlin. They were started by F. W. Marpurg, but completed and supplied with a preface and list of errors by C. P. E. Bach as editor. A second volume of 100 was issued by the same publisher in 1769. These were edited by J. F. Agricola, a son-in-law of J. S. Bach. The book was received with indignation by C. P. E. Bach in Hamburg, who proceeded to write an article condemning the new work in the *Staats- und Gelehrte Zeitung des Hamburgischen unpartheyeschen Correspondenten* on May 30, 1769. He claimed that the volume was full of mistakes and even contained chorales not composed by his father.

Beginning in April, 1777, and continuing for several years, Kirnberger started an active campaign to induce Breitkopf to publish the "complete" set of chorale harmonizations by J. S. Bach. His letters form an extremely interesting episode in this history, emphasizing as they do his desire to have the chorales published for the benefit of generations to come. The manuscript to be used once belonged to C. P. E. Bach, who sold it to the music-loving Princess Amalia through Kirnberger for twelve *louis d'or*. The greatest calamity in the history of these chorales is that the one who made this collection of chorales in manuscript did not think to include the texts and perhaps some reference to the larger work from which each chorale was taken. With the benefit of modern research these texts would have been of immeasurable assistance in present-day study. Just after Kirnberger died in 1783 without seeing the fruit of his labors, C. P. E. Bach was induced by Breitkopf to undertake the editing of these chorales. He accomplished the work in four parts, one part appearing in each of the following years: 1784, chorales 1-96; 1785, chorales 97-194; 1786, chorales 195-

283; 1787, chorales 283-370. This edition was republished as a *"neue Auflage"* in 1804 and possibly accounts for the missing *"zweite Auflage"*. In 1831 the so-called *"dritte Auflage"* mentioned above was published by Breitkopf & Härtel. C. F. Becker was called upon after the music was in type to write the preface. Attention has previously been called to the change of format and the change in the numbering beginning with No. 283. Since that time the edition has gone through untold printings and was published by a new process as the *"vierte Auflage"* in 1885 under the editorship of C. F. Becker and A. Dörffel. Another edition was sponsored by E. Naumann in 1897.

That C. P. E. Bach's edition, issued so early, should have faults and shortcomings can readily be understood in view of the lack of critical editorial standards existing at the time. Erk, in his splendid edition of the chorales issued by Peters in two volumes in 1850 and 1865 respectively, calls attention to these errors in such a comprehensive manner that they need not be enumerated here.

Again in 1841 C. F. Becker edited the chorales and had them published by Robert Friese of Leipzig. This edition was, in a way, an advance over previous publications since a return to the manner used by J. S. Bach himself in writing the chorales was undertaken. They were published in open score and in the original C-clefs, as they had appeared in J. S. Bach's own scores. For some reason, however, Becker chose to publish all of the harmonizations of the same melody in the same key. Since this called for transposition, it threw the range of the voices out of their natural limits and made the chorales worthless for singing. He, moreover, did not think of adding the words. Owing to these faults his edition was almost useless for practical purposes.

An important contribution was made by Ludwig C. Erk in his two volumes published by C. F. Peters in 1850 and 1865. Erk's work was accomplished largely before the advent of the Bachgesellschaft and represents a tremendous task of scholarly research. To his credit it should be stated that, influenced mainly by Rochlitz, he recognized the rôle that the text had played in the composition of the chorales. He therefore supplied the text to the chorales taken from all of the larger works that could still be located. Later he attempted to supply the missing words to those chorales taken from the larger works which had been lost. His work here was very valuable, but modern investigation based upon the methods of André Pirro should be able to improve upon his efforts to a very large extent. Erk's very excellent edition was thoroughly revised by Friedrich Smend in 1932 and republished by Peters.

The work of the Bachgesellschaft in publishing the compositions of Bach was a tremendous and heroic task. In this great edition every chorale of which the originally associated words are known was given its natural place in the larger composition of which it formed a part. This left 185 chorales that found no place because the works to which they originally belonged had been lost. Dr. Franz Wüllner collected these on the basis of their publication in the 1784-1787 edition, and issued them in Volume XXXIX of the Bachgesellschaft edition. He also included the melodies with figured bass. His work does not represent any particular advance over the researches of Erk.

When Breitkopf & Härtel published its edition of Bach for practical purposes, Dr. B. F. Richter edited the chorales. This edition consisted of 389 harmonized chorales supplied with texts based largely upon the work of Erk.

Waldemar Bargiel returned to the original form of the chorales in 1891 when Bote & Bock published in eight pamphlet volumes the chorales in the original open score and C-clefs. He had in mind furnishing material for score-reading for the classes of the Hochschule für Musik at Berlin. The edition is an excellent one, and texts are furnished as far as they could be passed upon as authentic. References to the place of each chorale in its larger work were also supplied. In this edition he included the melodies with figured bass.

An interesting work is that edited by H. Elliot Button and published a few years ago by Novello and Company, Ltd., London. It contains a valuable melodic index by means of which any chorale may be identified. No words were supplied for this edition.

A man to whom modern Bach research owes much is Dr. Charles Sanford Terry. His three-volume work on the Bach chorales, published by the Cambridge University Press in 1915, 1917, and 1921, contains extremely valuable information on sources and other details concerning the melodies and the hymns. His *J. S. Bach's Original Hymn-Tunes* is also a valuable contribution to this subject.

His latest work, *J. S. Bach's Four-Part Chorales*, published by the Oxford University Press in 1929, is perhaps the most comprehensive work covering the subject of the chorales. The book contains 405 harmonized chorales and 95 melodies with figured bass. They appear in short score. For each harmonization, Dr. Terry has furnished several stanzas of the hymn, both in the original German and in English translation. Among these is, of course, the original stanza which in each case is indicated by an asterisk. In furnishing these additional stanzas, Dr. Terry has proceeded upon the assumption that the Bach chorales are hymn-tunes for congregational use at religious services. It is very doubtful whether this assumption is correct. With the exception of the Schemelli songs, which were never harmonized for general use, and possibly a few other melodies, Bach never intended that the chorales should be sung by the congregation —at least in harmonized versions. His congregations knew the melodies of these chorales, and it is possible that they might have attempted to sing the melodies at the performances of the church cantatas and other works; but the harmonized versions of the chorales as we know them were not furnished the congregation— they were given only to his chorus. It is doubtful if the Bach chorales in great number would form ideal music for a congregation to sing. A few should be included in every hymnal worthy of the name, but the use of Bach's complete chorales as a congregational hymn-book is as far from their true function as was the total lack of words in the earlier editions.

There are numerous other selections of J. S. Bach's chorales issued by various publishers. They are largely only compilations for practical use and contain very little of information or further research.

However, one collection, complete in that it contains at least one example of each of J. S. Bach's chorales to which the original text is still known, should be mentioned. It is published by G. Schirmer, Inc., and was edited by Dr. Charles N. Boyd and the writer. It was compiled for the educational work of the National Association of Schools of Music and is primarily designed to supply material for score reading. It appears in two volumes. The first contains 91 chorales of the motet type; and the second, 29 chorales with independent orchestra *obbligato*. The chorales appear in open score using the original C-clefs and also in close score using the familiar treble and bass clefs.

The matter of translations of the Bach texts has been the *bête-noire* of every choir director. The difficulty of reproducing in exact words the idiomatic expressions of two different languages, the poetic licenses usually taken in translating verse, and the colloquial and antiquated expressions of the original version have been excellent reasons for translators to stray from the straight and narrow path. When it is taken into consideration that often a certain word is definitely illuminated by a certain harmony placed simultaneously with the word, one is not surprised to find, by reason of poetic license, the harmony and word separated by several beats or even several measures in the translation. For this reason, a thorough study of the relation of words and music should be made with the original text at hand. In the last named edition the editors have attempted to furnish a text most true to the original, both in meaning and placement of the words. To this end thirty original translations had to be made for the first book alone, and it was the hope of the editors to furnish a reliable assistance to those who are not able to master the finer intricacies of the German text, which is often very involved. It is recommended, however, that the original text be consulted for purposes of exact research.

In the notes at the end of the present collection will be found data valuable for a detailed examination of the chorales in this volume. It is the hope of the writer that these details will be the means of inspiring students to independent study with a consequently deepened understanding of these masterpieces, which may aptly be described as *multum in parvo*.

ALBERT RIEMENSCHNEIDER, Mus. D.
Director, Baldwin-Wallace Conservatory

INDEX OF THE CHORALES
ACCORDING TO PAGE

IN THIS INDEX the English line given beneath each chorale-name is merely a literal translation of the words standing above it. In several instances it seemed desirable to translate also a word or phrase farther along in the original text. When that has been done, the resulting supplementary English words or phrases have been set in italics. In none of the entries does the English line pretend to represent a translation for singing purposes. References to good singing translations will be found on pages 113 to 162.

An index to the 371 Chorales according to their *number* in the collection will be found on page 110.

Page

Ach bleib bei uns, Herr Jesu Christ....... 40
Ah, stay with us, Lord Jesus Christ
Ach, dass nicht die letzte Stunde........ 104
O that, *my life's* final hour *may* not *strike today!*
Ach Gott, erhör' mein Seufzen.......... 42
Ah, God, hear my sighing
Ach Gott und Herr, wie gross und schwer .10, 68
Ah, God and Lord, how great and heavy *my sins*
Ach Gott, vom Himmel sieh' darein...1, 62, 64
Ah, God, from heaven look therein *and be merciful*
Ach Gott, wie manches Herzeleid....36, 52, 75
Ah, God, full many a heartbreak
Ach lieben Christen, seid getrost... ......8, 73
Ah, dear Christians, be comforted
Ach was soll ich Sünder machen.......... 10
Ah, what am I, a sinner, to do
Ach wie nichtig, ach wie flüchtig......... 11
Ah, how empty! ah, how fleeting!
Allein Gott in der Höh' sei Ehr'..29, 60, 76, 79
Only to God on high be glory!
Allein zu dir, Herr Jesu Christ...........4, 87
Only in Thee, Lord Jesus Christ
Alle Menschen müssen sterben............ 35
All men must die
Alles ist an Gottes Segen................ 29
Everything is on God's blessing *dependent*
Als der gütige Gott..................... 37
When merciful God
Als Jesus Christus in der Nacht.......... 41
When Jesus Christ in the night
Als vierzig Tag' nach Ostern.... 49
When forty days after Easter
An Wasserflüssen Babylon............... 2
By the rivers of Babylon
Auf, auf! die rechte Zeit ist hier.......... 93
Up, up, the proper time is here
Auf, auf! mein Herz, mit Freuden........ 97
Up, up, my heart, with joy

Page

Auf, auf, mein Herz, und du mein ganzer
Sinn................................ 28
Up, up, my heart, and thou my entire being
Auf meinen lieben Gott................. 74
In my dear God
Aus meines Herzens Grunde............. 1
From the depths of my heart
Aus tiefer Not schrei' ich zu dir.......... 4
From deep need I cry to Thee
Befiehl du deine Wege.........66, 70, 82, 89
Entrust thy ways
Beglückter Stand getreuer Seelen......... 100
Blessed state of faithful souls
Beschränkt, ihr Weisen dieser Welt....... 102
Confine, ye wise men of this world, *your friendship*
Brich entzwei, mein armes Herze........ 96
Break in twain, my poor heart
Brunnquell aller Güter.................. 98
Fountainhead of all virtues
Christ, der du bist der helle Tag.......... 55
Christ, Who art clear day
Christe, der du bist Tag und Licht........ 59
Christ, Who art day and light
Christe, du Beistand deiner Kreuzgemeine. 50
Christ, Thou support of Thy followers
Christ ist erstanden.................... 45
Christ is risen
Christ lag in Todesbanden........5, 42, 64, 90
Christ lay in the bonds of death
Christum wir sollen loben schon........ 13
Let us be praising Christ
Christ, unser Herr, zum Jordan kam....15, 27
Christ our Lord came to the Jordan
Christus, der ist mein Leben............2, 77
Christ is my life
Christus, der uns selig macht....19, 26, 45, 75
Christ, Who makes us blessed

Page

Christus ist erstanden, hat überwunden.... 46
Christ is risen, has conquered

Da der Herr Christ zu Tische sass........ 44
As Lord Christ was at supper

Danket dem Herren, denn er ist sehr freundlich................................ 55
Thank ye the Lord, for He is very gracious

Dank sei Gott in der Höhe.............. 76
Thanks be to God on high

Das alte Jahr vergangen ist...........37, 76
The old year has passed away

Das neugeborne Kindelein.............12, 41
The new-born Babe

Das walt' Gott Vater und Gott Sohn...... 54
God the Father and God the Son grant it!

Das walt' mein Gott................... 17
My Lord grant it!

Den Vater dort oben 58
The Father there above

Der du bist drei in Einigkeit............. 36
Thou Who art three in unity

Der Herr ist mein getreuer Hirt.......... 85
The Lord is my faithful shepherd

Der lieben Sonnen Licht und Pracht...... 91
The dear sun's light and splendor

Der Tag, der ist so freudenreich.......... 36
This day is so joyful

Der Tag ist hin, die Sonne gehet nieder.... 92
Day is done; the sun is setting

Der Tag mit seinem Lichte............. 92
Day with its light

Des heil'gen Geistes reiche Gnad'......... 49
The Holy Ghost's abundant mercy

Dich bet' ich an, mein höchster Gott...... 98
I worship Thee, my God most high

Die bittre Leidenszeit beginnet........... 95
Bitter Passion-tide begins

Die goldne Sonne, voll Freud' und Wonne.. 91
The golden sun, full of joy and gladness

Die Nacht ist kommen................. 55
Night has come

Die Sonn' hat sich mit ihrem Glanz....... 56
The sun in its splendor has set

Dies sind die heil'gen zehn Gebot'........ 29
These are the sacred ten commandments

Dir, dir, Jehovah, will ich singen......49, 98
To Thee, Thee, Jehovah, I will sing

Du Friedensfürst, Herr Jesu Christ........ 10
Thou Prince of Peace, Lord Jesus Christ

Du grosser Schmerzensmann............. 38
Thou great Man of Sorrow

Du Lebensfürst, Herr Jesu Christ........ 87
Thou Prince of Life, Lord Jesus Christ

Page

Du, o schönes Weltgebäude............ 20, 31
Thou, O fair universe

Durch Adams Fall ist ganz verderbt.... 23, 29
Adam's fall entirely corrupted human nature.

Ein' feste Burg ist unser Gott....... 6, 61, 66
A stronghold is our God

Ein Lämmlein geht und trägt die Schuld... 75
A Lambkin goes and bears the guilt

Eins ist not! ach Herr, dies Eine....... 68, 93
One thing is needful, O Lord, this one thing

Erbarm' dich mein, o Herre Gott........ 9
Have mercy on me, O Lord God

Erhalt' uns, Herr, bei deinem Wort....... 17
Preserve us, Lord, by Thy word

Ermuntre dich, mein schwacher Geist 3, 23, 94
Rouse thyself, my weak spirit

Erschienen ist der herrliche Tag......... 5
The glorious day has dawned

Erstanden ist der heil'ge Christ.......... 40
Blessed Christ hath risen

Erwürgtes Lamm, das die.............. 101
Slaughtered Lamb

Es glänzet der Christen inwendiges Leben. 101
The inner life of the Christians is shining

Es ist das Heil uns kommen her.... 2, 70, 81
Salvation has come to us

Es ist genug; so nimm, Herr............. 52
It is enough! So take, Lord

Es ist gewisslich an der Zeit........... 63, 88
It is certainly time

Es ist nun aus mit meinem Leben........ 104
My life is now almost gone

Es ist vollbracht! vergiss ja nicht........ 97
It is fulfilled; do not forget

Es kostet viel, ein Christ zu sein......... 100
It takes much sacrifice to be a Christian

Es spricht der Unweisen Mund.......... 7
The lips of the foolish say

Es stehn vor Gottes Throne............. 38
There stand before God's throne

Es wird schier der letzte Tag............ 57
The final day will soon arrive

Es woll' uns Gott genädig sein.......5, 80, 85
May God be merciful to us

Freu' dich sehr, o meine Seele.... 8, 15, 18, 69
Rejoice greatly, O my soul

Freuet euch, ihr Christen alle.......... 3
Rejoice, ye Christians all

Für deinen Thron tret' ich hiermit........ 81
Before Thy throne I herewith come

Für Freuden lasst uns springen.......... 37
Let us leap with joy

Page

Gelobet seist du, Jesu Christ....... 12, 37, 70
Praised be Thou, Jesus Christ
Gib dich zufrieden und sei stille........66, 102
Be content and be silent
Gott, der du selber bist das Licht......... 54
God, Who art Thyself the light
Gott der Vater wohn' uns bei............ 31
God the Father, dwell with us
Gott des Himmels und der Erden......... 9
God of heaven and of earth
Gottes Sohn ist kommen................ 5
The Son of God has come
Gott hat das Evangelium................ 41
God gave the Gospel
Gott lebet noch..................... 56, 100
God still lives
Gottlob, es geht nunmehr zu Ende........ 44
Thank God, it now is almost over
Gott sei gelobet und gebenedeiet.......... 16
God be praised and blessed
Gott sei uns gnädig und barmherzig....... 78
God be gracious and merciful to us
Gott, wie gross ist deine Güte............ 98
God, how great Thy goodness is!

Hast du denn, Jesu, dein Angesicht...... 21
Hast Thou then, Jesus, hidden Thy countenance
Heilig, heilig........................ 57
Holy, holy
Helft mir Gott's Güte preisen...... 20, 23, 28
Help me praise God's goodness
Herr Christ, der ein'ge Gott'ssohn...... 23, 74
Lord Christ, the only Son of God
Herr Gott, dich loben alle wir............ 38
Lord God, we all praise Thee
Herr Gott, dich loben wir............... 48
Lord God, we praise Thee
Herr, ich denk' an jene Zeit............. 50
Lord, I am thinking of that time
Herr, ich habe missgehandelt........... 8, 70
Lord, I have transgressed
Herr Jesu Christ, dich zu uns wend'....... 32
Lord Jesus Christ, turn towards us
Herr Jesu Christ, du hast bereit.......... 54
Lord Jesus Christ, Thou hast already
Herr Jesu Christ, du höchstes Gut. 17, 65, 71
Lord Jesus Christ, Thou highest good
Herr Jesu Christ, mein's Lebens Licht..... 71
Lord Jesus Christ, light of my life
Herr Jesu Christ, wahr'r Mensch und Gott 43, 69
Lord Jesus Christ, true Man and God
Herr, nicht schicke deine Rache.......... 92
Lord, send not Thy vengeance

Page

Herr, nun lass in Frieden................ 43
Lord, permit now in peace Thy servant to depart
Herr, straf mich nicht in deinem Zorn..... 53
Lord, punish me not in Thy wrath
Herr, wie du willst, so schick's mit mir.... 77
Lord, ordain what Thou wilt for me
Herzlich lieb hab' ich dich, o Herr... 13, 24, 67
Dearly I love Thee, O Lord
Herzlich tut mich verlangen.............. 6
I desire sincerely a blessed ending
Herzliebster Jesu, was hast du.... 14, 18, 24, 25
Dearest Jesus, how hast Thou transgressed
Heut' ist, o Mensch, ein grosser.......... 39
This day, O mortal, is a great day of sorrow
Heut' triumphieret Gottes Sohn.......... 18
Today God's Son triumphs
Hilf, Gott, dass mir's gelinge........... 46, 73
Help me, God, to succeed
Hilf, Herr Jesu, lass gelingen........... 36, 89
Help, Lord Jesus, send good speed!

Ich bin ja, Herr, in deiner Macht...... 61, 105
I am indeed, Lord, in Thy power
Ich dank' dir, Gott, für all' Wohltat....... 53
I thank Thee, God, for all Thy benefits
Ich dank' dir, lieber Herre........... 1, 66, 82
I thank Thee, dear Lord
Ich dank' dir schon durch deinen Sohn.... 43
I thank Thee, indeed, through Thy Son
Ich danke dir, o Gott, in deinem Throne... 55
I thank Thee, O God upon Thy throne
Ich freue mich in dir.................. 14, 94
I rejoice in Thee
Ich hab' in Gottes Herz und Sinn......... 84
I have in God's heart and mind
Ich hab' mein' Sach' Gott heimgestellt.... 6
I have placed all my affairs in God's hands
Ich halte treulich still.................. 102
I shall remain faithfully silent
Ich lass' dich nicht.................... 103
I shall not leave Thee
Ich liebe Jesum alle Stund'.............. 103
I love Jesus always
Ich ruf' zu dir, Herr Jesu Christ.......... 17
I call to Thee, Lord Jesus Christ
Ich steh' an deiner Krippen hier.......... 94
I stand here by Thy crib
Ihr Gestirn', ihr hohlen Lüfte.......... 37, 94
Ye stars, ye airy winds
In allen meinen Taten................. 12, 33
In all my deeds
In dich hab' ich gehoffet, Herr......... 18, 27
On Thee I have set my hope, O Lord

Page

In dulci jubilo........................ 33
   In sweet jubilation
Ist Gott mein Schild und Helfersmann.... 28
   If God is my shield and helper

Jesu, deine tiefen Wunden.............. 62
   Jesus, Thy deep wounds
Jesü, deine Liebeswunden.............. 93
   Jesus, Thy dear wounds
Jesu, der du meine Seele........ 9, 65, 72, 90
   Jesus, Thou Who *saved* my soul
Jesu, der du selbsten wohl.............. 39
   Jesus, Thou Who Thyself indeed *hast tasted death*
Jesu, du mein liebstes Leben............ 59
   Jesus, Thou my dearest life
Jesu ist das schönste Licht.............. 99
   Jesus is the fairest light
Jesu, Jesu, du bist mein............. 59, 104
   Jesus, Jesus, Thou art mine
Jesu Leiden, Pein und Tod....... 14, 19, 24
   Jesus' suffering, pain, and death
Jesu, meine Freude...... 22, 32, 64, 69, 78, 86
   Jesus, my joy
Jesu, meiner Seelen Wonne........... 84, 88
   Jesus, joy of my soul
Jesu, meines Glaubens Zier............. 93
   Jesus, ornament of my faith
Jesu, meines Herzens Freud'......... 64, 103
   Jesus, joy of my heart
Jesu, nun sei gepreiset............. 4, 61, 79
   Jesus now be praised
Jesus Christus, unser Heiland.......... 8, 40
   Jesus Christ, our Savior
Jesus, meine Zuversicht.............. 40, 81
   Jesus, my confidence
Jesus, unser Trost und Leben............ 97
   Jesus, our comfort and life

Keinen hat Gott verlassen.............. 29
   God hath forsaken no one
Kein Stündlein geht dahin.............. 105
   No brief hour vanishes
Komm, Gott Schöpfer, heiliger Geist...... 43
   Come, God the Creator, Holy Ghost
Komm, heiliger Geist, Herre Gott........ 16
   Come, Holy Ghost, Lord God
Komm, süsser Tod, komm sel'ge........ 105
   Come, sweet Death! Come, blessed *Rest*
Kommt her zu mir, spricht Gottes Sohn .. 11, 90
   "Come to me," speaks the Son of God
Kommt, Seelen, dieser Tag............. 107
   Brethren, when this day comes
Kommt wieder aus der finstern Gruft..... 107
   Come again from out the dark tomb

Page

Kyrie, Gott Vater in Ewigkeit........... 30
   Kyrie, God the Father eternally

Lass, o Herr, dein Ohr sich neigen....... 52
   Bow Thine ear, O Lord
Lasset uns mit Jesu ziehen.............. 95
   Let us go with Jesus
Liebes Herz, bedenke doch.............. 99
   Dear heart, consider yet
Liebster Gott, wann werd' ich sterben.. 10, 105
   Dearest God, when shall I die
Liebster Herr Jesu! wo bleibest.......... 106
   Dearest Lord Jesus, where art Thou remaining
Liebster Jesu, wir sind hier............ 30, 79
   Dearest Jesus, we are here
Liebster Immanuel, Herzog der From-
men.......................... 44, 104
   Dearest Immanuel, Lord of the devout
Lobet den Herren, denn er ist sehr freund-
lich............................... 54
   Praise the Lord, for He is most gracious
Lobt Gott, ihr Christen, allzugleich. 13, 67, 82
   Praise God, ye Christians, all together

Mach's mit mir, Gott, nach deiner Güt'. 11, 75
   Do with me as Thy goodness prompts Thee
Meine Augen schliess' ich jetzt........... 63
   Now I close my eyes
Meinen Jesum lass' ich nicht, Jesus....... 35
   I will not leave my Jesus; Jesus *will not leave me*
Meinen Jesum lass' ich nicht, weil. 35, 73, 84
   I will not leave my Jesus, since *He gave Himself*
Meine Seele erhebet den Herrn........ 29, 87
   My soul exalts the Lord
Meines Lebens letzte Zeit............ 83, 106
   The last hour of my life
Mein Jesu, dem die Seraphinen........... 93
   My Jesus, Whom the seraphim *serve*
Mein Jesu! was für Seelenweh........... 95
   My Jesus, how great anguish of soul
Mit Fried' und Freud' ich fahr' dahin... 12, 79
   With peace and joy I journey thither
Mitten wir im Leben sind.............. 51
   In the midst of life, we are *surrounded by death*

Nicht so traurig, nicht so sehr........ 35, 101
   Not so sadly, not so deeply *troubled*
Nimm von uns, Herr, du treuer Gott...... 71
   Avert from us, Lord, Thou faithful God, *the punishment*
Nun bitten wir den heiligen Geist.... 9, 19, 22
   Now let us beg *true faith* of the Holy Ghost
Nun danket alle Gott.................. 8, 80
   Now let all thank God

Page

Nun freut euch, Gottes Kinder all'........ 42
Now rejoice, all ye children of God

Nun freut euch, lieben Christen, g'mein.... 42
Now rejoice, dear Christians, together

Nun komm, der Heiden Heiland........ 7, 39
Now come, Savior of the Gentiles

Nun lasst uns Gott, dem Herren........ 62
Now let us to God the Lord *give thanks*

Nun lieget alles unter dir............... 83
Now all lies beneath Thee

Nun lob', mein' Seel', den Herren. 2, 26, 65, 72
Now praise the Lord, my soul

Nun preiset alle Gottes Barmherzigkeit.. 53
Now let all praise God's mercy

Nun ruhen alle Wälder..... 14, 23, 27, 70, 86
Now all the forests are at rest

Nun sich der Tag geendet hat........... 58
When now the day is at an end

Nur mein Jesus ist mein Leben........... 103
Only my Jesus is my life

O du Liebe meiner Liebe............... 96
O Thou Love of my love

O Ewigkeit, du Donnerwort............ 7, 67
O Eternity, thou word of thunder

O finstre Nacht, wenn wirst du........... 106
O gloomy night, when wilt thou

O Gott, du frommer Gott....... 20, 76, 77, 81
O God, Thou good God

O grosser Gott von Macht............... 19
O great God of might

O Haupt voll Blut und Wunden 17, 18, 20, 22, 83
O Head, bloody and wounded

O Herre Gott, dein göttlich Wort......... 5
O Lord our God, Thy holy word

O Herzensangst, o Bangigkeit............ 40
O anguish of heart! O fear!

O Jesu Christ, du höchstes Gut........... 21
O Jesus Christ, Thou highest good

O Jesu, du mein Bräutigam............... 57
O Jesus, Thou my bridegroom

O Jesulein süss, o Jesulein mild........ 94
O sweet Child Jesus, O gentle Child Jesus

O Lamm Gottes, unschuldig............. 38
O Lamb of God, innocent

O liebe Seele, zieh die Sinnen............ 101
O beloved soul, turn your senses *away from desires*

O Mensch, bewein' dein' Sünde gross.. 46, 74
O Man, bewail thy great sins

O Mensch, schau Jesum Christum an...... 47
O Man, behold Jesus Christ

O Traurigkeit, o Herzeleid............. 13
O sadness, O bitter pain

Page

O Welt, sieh hier dein Leben........ 67, 88, 89
O World, behold thy life

O wie selig seid ihr doch, ihr Frommen 50, 52, 106
O how blessed ye are, ye faithful

O wir armen Sünder.................... 47
O we poor sinners

Puer natus in Bethlehem................. 4
A Boy born in Bethlehem

Sanctus, Sanctus Dominus Deus Sabaoth.. 77
Holy, holy, Lord God of Sabaoth

Schaut, ihr Sünder..................... 39
Behold, ye sinners

Schmücke dich, o liebe Seele............. 6
Deck thyself, dear soul

Schwing' dich auf zu deinem Gott......... 33
Soar upwards to thy God

Seelen-Bräutigam..................... 33, 99
Bridegroom of the soul

Seelenweide, meine Freude............... 103
Pasture for the soul, my Joy

Sei gegrüsset, Jesu gütig............... 39, 96
Hail to Thee, Jesus kind

Sei Lob und Ehr' dem höchsten Gut.. 60, 79, 86
Praise and honor to the highest Good!

Selig! wer an Jesum denkt............... 96
Blessed, he who thinks on Jesus!

Singen wir aus Herzens Grund............ 25
Let us sing from the depths of our hearts

Singt dem Herrn ein neues Lied........... 60
Sing the Lord a new song

So gehst du nun, mein Jesu, hin.......... 96
Thus goest Thou now, my Jesus, thither

So gibst du nun, mein Jesu, gute Nacht. 49, 97
Must Thou now thus, my Jesus, say good-night

Sollt' ich meinem Gott nicht singen....... 53
Am I not to sing to my God

So wünsch ich mir zu guter.............. 107
Thus *at last* I wish *to die in peace*

Straf' mich nicht in deinem Zorn......... 9
Punish me not in Thy wrath

Steh ich bei meinem Gott................ 107
If I stand by my God

Uns ist ein Kindlein heut' gebor'n........ 34
A Child is born to us this day

Valet will ich dir geben................ 7, 25
I wish to bid you farewell

Vater unser im Himmelreich....... 11, 25, 65
Our Father, Who art in heaven

Verleih' uns Frieden gnädiglich..... 21, 51, 63
Mercifully grant us peace

Page

Vergiss mein nicht, dass ich dein nicht ver-
    gesse 99
    Forget me not, that I may not forget Thee
Vergiss mein nicht, vergiss mein nicht 102
    Forget me not, forget me not
Vom Himmel hoch, da komm' ich her . . . 11, 83
    From heaven above I hither come
Von Gott will ich nicht lassen . . 26, 43, 80, 88
    From God I will not depart

Wach' auf, mein Herz, und singe 21
    Awake, my heart, and sing
Wachet auf, ruft uns die Stimme 41
    "Awake!" the voice is calling to us
Wär' Gott nicht mit uns diese Zeit 42, 69
    If God were not with us this time
Warum betrübst du dich, mein Herz . 22, 34, 73
    Why do you grieve, my heart?
Warum sollt' ich mich denn grämen 32, 86
    Why should I then grieve?
Was betrübst du dich, mein Herze 57
    What makes you grieve, my heart?
Was bist du doch, o Seele, so betrübet . . 44, 104
    Why art thou yet, O soul, so troubled?
Was frag' ich nach der Welt 62, 71
    Why do I ask for the world
Was Gott tut, das ist wohlgetan 15, 71, 84
    What God does is well done
Was mein Gott will, das g'scheh' . 10, 26, 27, 64
    May what my God wills come to pass
Was willst du dich, o meine Seele 58
    Why do you wish, O my soul, to feel grieved
Weg, mein Herz, mit den Gedanken 62, 72
    Away, my heart, with the thoughts
Welt, ade! ich bin dein müde 35
    World, adieu! I am tired of thee
Weltlich Ehr' und zeitlich Gut 50
    Worldly honor and temporal good

Page

Wenn ich in Angst und Not 34
    When I in anxiety and need
Wenn mein Stündlein vorhanden ist 12, 78, 85
    When my brief hour is come
Wenn wir in höchsten Nöten sein 16, 60
    When we are in utmost need
Werde munter, mein Gemüte 22, 28, 56
    Be glad, my soul
Wer Gott vertraut, hat wohl gebaut 32
    He who trusts God has built well
Wer in dem Schutz des Höchsten ist 34
    He who is in the protection of the Highest
Wer nur den lieben Gott lässt 14, 24, 25, 34, 82
    He who lets only beloved God rule
Wer weiss, wie nahe mir mein Ende 47
    Who knows how near my end may be
Wie bist du, Seele, in mir so gar betrübt . . . 59
    Why art thou, soul, so troubled within me
Wie schön leuchtet der Morgenstern
                        20, 44, 68, 74, 78
    How brightly shines the morning star
Wir Christenleut' 13, 78, 87
    We Christian folk
Wir glauben all' an einen Gott, Schöpfer . . 31
    We all believe in one God, the Creator
Wo Gott der Herr nicht bei uns hält 81
    Had God the Lord not remained with us
Wo Gott zum Haus nicht gibt sein' Gunst . 36
    If God does not bestow His grace
Wo ist mein Schäflein, das ich liebe 92
    Where is my lamb, which I love
Wo soll ich fliehen hin 7, 68, 80
    Whither am I to flee?

Zeuch ein zu deinen Toren 6
    Enter Thy gates

JOHANN SEBASTIAN BACH
371 Harmonized Chorales

Revised, corrected, edited, and annotated by
Albert Riemenschneider*

*The previous publications of the 371—even the latest of them—contain numerous inaccuracies, which have been corrected in this **edition.**
Those chorales in which corrections have been made (beyond the mere removal of meaningless slurs) are marked with asterisks.

2

Es ist das Heil uns kommen her*

4.

An Wasserflüssen Babylon

5.

Christus, der ist mein Leben

6.

Nun lob', mein' Seel', den Herren

7.

Freuet euch, ihr Christen*

8.

Ermuntre dich, mein schwacher Geist*

9.

4

Aus tiefer Not schrei' ich zu dir *

10.

Jesu, nun sei gepreiset

11.

Puer natus in Bethlehem

12.

Allein zu dir, Herr Jesu Christ *

13.

6

Ich hab' mein' Sach' Gott heimgestellt

19.

Ein' feste Burg ist unser Gott

20.

Herzlich tut mich verlangen

21.

Schmücke dich, o liebe Seele

22.

Zeuch ein zu deinen Toren*

23.

12

24. Valet will ich dir geben

25. Wo soll ich fliehen hin

26. O Ewigkeit, du Donnerwort

27. Es spricht der Unweisen Mund

28. Nun komm, der Heiden Heiland*

8

Freu' dich sehr, o meine Seele *

29.

Jesus Christus, unser Heiland

30.

Ach lieben Christen, seid getrost

31.

Nun danket alle Gott

32.

Herr, ich habe mißgehandelt

33.

Erbarm' dich mein, o Herre Gott

Gott des Himmels und der Erden *

Nun bitten wir den heiligen Geist

Jesu, der du meine Seele

Straf' mich nicht in deinem Zorn

Mach's mit mir, Gott, nach deiner Güt'

44.

Kommt her zu mir, spricht *

45.

Vom Himmel hoch, da komm' ich her *

46.

Vater unser im Himmelreich

47.

Ach wie nichtig, ach wie flüchtig *

48.

Mit Fried' und Freud' ich fahr' dahin

49.

In allen meinen Taten

50.

Gelobet seist du, Jesu Christ*

51.

Wenn mein Stündlein vorhanden ist

52.

Das neugeborne Kindelein*

53.

Lobt Gott, ihr Christen, allzugleich

54.

Wir Christenleut'

55.

Christum wir sollen loben schon*

56.

O Traurigkeit

57.

Herzlich lieb hab' ich dich, o Herr

58.

14

59. Herzliebster Jesu, was hast du*

60. Ich freue mich in dir

61. Jesu Leiden, Pein und Tod*

62. Wer nur den lieben Gott läßt walten*

63. Nun ruhen alle Wälder

Freu' dich sehr, o meine Seele

64.

Was Gott tut, das ist wohlgetan

65.

Christ, unser Herr, zum Jordan kam

66.

Freu' dich sehr, o meine Seele

67.

Wenn wir in höchsten Nöten sein

68.

Komm, heiliger Geist, Herre Gott

69.

Gott sei gelobet und gebenedeiet

70.

18

Freu' dich sehr, o meine Seele*

76.

In dich hab' ich gehoffet, Herr*

77.

Herzliebster Jesu, was hast du*

78.

Heut' triumphieret Gottes Sohn

79.

O Haupt voll Blut und Wunden

80.

Christus, der uns selig macht

81.

O großer Gott von Macht*

82.

Jesu Leiden, Pein und Tod*

83.

Nun bitten wir den heiligen Geist

84.

O Gott, du frommer Gott *

85.

Wie schön leuchtet der Morgenstern *

86.

Du, o schönes Weltgebäude *

87.

Helft mir Gott's Güte preisen

88.

O Haupt voll Blut und Wunden *

89.

Hast du denn, Jesu, dein Angesicht

90.

Verleih' uns Frieden gnädiglich *

91.

O Jesu Christ, du höchstes Gut

92.

Wach' auf, mein Herz

93.

Warum betrübst du dich, mein Herz*

94.

Werde munter, mein Gemüte

95.

Jesu, meine Freude*

96.

Nun bitten wir den heiligen Geist*

97.

O Haupt voll Blut und Wunden*

98.

Helft mir Gott's Güte preisen *

99.

Durch Adams Fall ist ganz verderbt

100.

Herr Christ, der ein'ge Gott's-Sohn

101.

Ermuntre dich, mein schwacher Geist *

102.

Nun ruhen alle Wälder *

103.

24

Wer nur den lieben Gott läßt walten*

104.

Herzliebster Jesu, was hast du verbrochen*

105.

Jesu Leiden, Pein und Tod

106.

Herzlich lieb hab' ich dich, o Herr

107.

Valet will ich dir geben*

108.

Singen wir aus Herzens Grund

109.

Vater unser im Himmelreich

110.

Herzliebster Jesu, was hast du verbrochen

111.

Wer nur den lieben Gott läßt walten

112.

Christus, der uns selig macht *

113.

Von Gott will ich nicht lassen

114.

Was mein Gott will, das

115.

Nun lob', mein' Seel', den Herren *

116.

117. Nun ruhen alle Wälder

118. In dich hab' ich gehoffet, Herr

119. Christ, unser Herr, zum Jordan kam*

120. Was mein Gott will, das g'scheh' allzeit

28

Werde munter, mein Gemüte *

121.

Ist Gott mein Schild und Helfersmann *

122.

Helft mir Gott's Güte preisen

123.

Auf, auf, mein Herz, und du mein ganzer Sinn

124.

Wir glauben all' an einen Gott

133.

Du, o schönes Weltgebäude

134.

Gott der Vater wohn' uns bei

135.

Herr Jesu Christ, dich zu uns wend'

136.

Wer Gott vertraut, hat wohl gebaut

137.

Jesu, meine Freude

138.

Warum sollt ich mich denn grämen *

139.

Wer in dem Schutz des Höchsten

144.

Warum betrübst du dich

145.

Wer nur den lieben Gott läßt walten

146.

Wenn ich in Angst und Not

147.

Uns ist ein Kindlein heut' gebor'n

148.

Nicht so traurig, nicht so sehr

149.

Welt, ade! ich bin dein müde *

150.

Meinen Jesum laß' ich nicht, Jesus

151.

Meinen Jesum laß' ich nicht, weil *

152.

Alle Menschen müssen sterben

153.

Der du bist drei in Einigkeit

Hilf, Herr Jesu, laß gelingen

Ach Gott, wie manches Herzeleid

Wo Gott zum Haus nicht gibt

Der Tag, der ist so freudenreich

Als der gütige Gott

159.

Gelobet seist du, Jesu Christ *

160.

Ihr Gestirn', ihr hohlen Lüfte

161.

Das alte Jahr vergangen ist

162.

Für Freuden laßt uns springen

163.

164. Herr Gott, dich loben alle wir

165. O Lamm Gottes, unschuldig

166. Es stehn vor Gottes Throne

167. Du großer Schmerzensmann

Heut' ist, o Mensch, ein großer

168.

Jesu, der du selbsten wohl

169.

Nun komm, der Heiden Heiland *

170.

Schaut, ihr Sünder

171.

Sei gegrüßet, Jesu gütig

172.

Das neugeborne Kindelein

178.

Wachet auf, ruft uns die Stimme *

179.

Als Jesus Christus in der Nacht

180.

Gott hat das Evangelium

181.

Wär' Gott nicht mit uns diese Zeit *

182.

183. Nun freut euch, lieben Christen, g'mein

184. Christ lag in Todesbanden *

185. Nun freut euch, Gottes Kinder all'

186. Ach Gott, erhör' mein Seufzen

Gottlob, es geht nunmehr zu Ende

192.

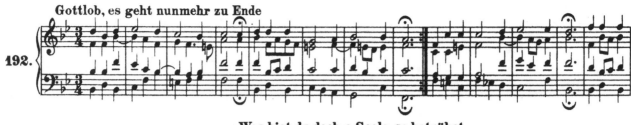

Was bist du doch, o Seele, so betrübet

193.

Liebster Immanuel, Herzog der Frommen*

194.

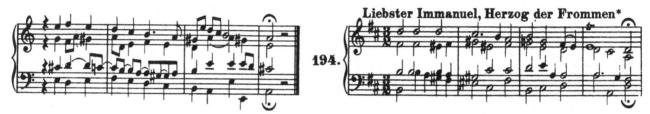

Wie schön leuchtet der Morgenstern

195.

Da der Herr Christ zu Tische saß

196.

Christ ist erstanden

197.

Wär er nicht erstanden

Alleluja

Christus, der uns selig macht

198.

Hilf, Gott, daß mir's gelinge

199.

Christus ist erstanden, hat überwunden

200.

O Mensch, bewein' dein' Sünde groß

201.

O wir armen Sünder

202.

O Mensch, schau Jesum Christum an

203.

Wer weiß, wie nahe mir *

204.

48

Herr Gott, dich loben wir

(three times)

205.

Heilig ist Gott
(two times)

Heilig

(six times)

Du König
(six times)

Laß uns im Himmel haben Teil

(three times)

Auf dich hoffen wir

So gibst du nun, mein Jesu, gute Nacht

206.

Des heil'gen Geistes reiche Gnad'

207.

Als vierzig Tag' nach Ostern

208.

Dir, dir, Jehovah, will ich singen

209.

Christe, du Beistand deiner Kreuzgemeine

210.

Weltlich Ehr' und zeitlich Gut

211.

Herr, ich denk' an jene Zeit

212.

O wie selig seid ihr doch, ihr Frommen

213.

Mitten wir im Leben sind

214.

Verleih' uns Frieden gnädiglich[*]

215.

Es ist genug; so nimm, Herr *

216.

Ach Gott, wie manches Herzeleid

217.

Laß, o Herr, dein Ohr sich neigen

218.

O wie selig seid ihr doch, ihr Frommen

219.

Das walt' Gott Vater und Gott Sohn

224.

225. Gott, der du selber bist das Licht

Herr Jesu Christ, du hast bereit

226.

Lobet den Herren, denn er ist sehr freundlich

227.

Danket dem Herren, denn er ist sehr freundlich

228.

Ich danke dir, o Gott, in deinem Throne

229.

Christ, der du bist der helle Tag

230.

Die Nacht ist kommen

231.

56

Die Sonn' hat sich mit ihrem Glanz

232.

Werde munter, mein Gemüte*

233.

Gott lebet noch

234.

Heilig, heilig

235.

O Jesu, du mein Bräutigam

236.

Was betrübst du dich, mein Herze

237.

Es wird schier der letzte Tag

238.

58

Den Vater dort oben

239.

Nun sich der Tag geendet hat

240.

Was willst du dich, o meine Seele

241.

Singt dem Herrn ein neues Lied

246.

Wenn wir in höchsten Nöten sein

247.

Sei Lob und Ehr' dem höchsten Gut

248.

Allein Gott in der Höh' sei Ehr'

249.

Ein' feste Burg ist unser Gott

250.

Ich bin ja, Herr, in deiner Macht

251.

Jesu, nun sei gepreiset

252.

62

Meine Augen schließ' ich jetzt

258.

Verleih' uns Frieden gnädiglich

259.

Es ist gewißlich an der Zeit

260.

261. Christ lag in Todesbanden

262. Ach Gott, vom Himmel sieh' darein *

263. Jesu, meine Freude

264. Jesu, meines Herzens Freud'

265. Was mein Gott will, das

Befiehl du deine Wege *

Flauto I & II

270.

Gib dich zufrieden und sei stille

271.

Ich dank' dir, lieber Herre

272.

Ein' feste Burg ist unser Gott *

273.

O Ewigkeit, du Donnerwort

274.

O Welt, sieh hier dein Leben

275.

Lobt Gott, ihr Christen, allzugleich

276.

Herzlich lieb hab'ich dich, o Herr

277.

67

Wie schön leuchtet der Morgenstern

278.

Ach Gott und Herr

279.

Eins ist not! ach Herr, dies Eine

280.

Wo soll ich fliehen hin*

281.

70

71

72

296. Nun lob', mein' Seel', den Herren

297. Jesu, der du meine Seele*

298. Weg, mein Herz, mit den Gedanken*

Meinen Jesum laß ich nicht

299.

Warum betrübst du dich, mein Herz

300.

Ach, lieben Christen, seid getrost

301.

Hilf, Gott, daß mir's gelinge

302.

Dank sei Gott in der Höhe

311.

O Gott, du frommer Gott*

312.

Allein Gott in der Höh' sei Ehr'*

313.

Corno II

(Cor. I)

(Cor. II)

Das alte Jahr vergangen ist

314.

O Gott, du frommer Gott

315.

Christus, der ist mein Leben

316.

Herr, wie du willst, so schick's mit mir*

317.

Herr, wie du willst, so schick's mit mir

318.

Sanctus, Sanctus Dominus Deus Sabaoth

319.

Gott sei uns gnädig und barmherzig

320.

Wir Christenleut'

321.

Wenn mein Stündlein vorhanden ist

322.

Wie schön leuchtet der Morgenstern *

323.

Jesu, meine Freude

324.

Für deinen Thron tret' ich hiermit

334.

Es ist das Heil uns kommen her *

335.

Wo Gott der Herr nicht bei uns hält

336.

O Gott, du frommer Gott

337.

Jesus, meine Zuversicht

338.

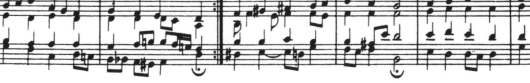

Nun lieget alles unter dir *

343.

Vom Himmel hoch, da komm' ich her *

344.

O Haupt voll Blut und Wunden*

345.

Meines Lebens letzte Zeit

346.

Was Gott tut, das ist wohlgetan*

347.

Meinen Jesum laß ich nicht*

348.

Ich hab' in Gottes Herz und Sinn

349.

Jesu, meiner Seelen Wonne

350.

Wenn mein Stündlein vorhanden ist

351.

Es woll' uns Gott genädig sein

352.

Der Herr ist mein getreuer Hirt*

353.

Sei Lob und Ehr' dem höchsten Gut[*]

354.

Nun ruhen alle Wälder

355.

Jesu, meine Freude

356.

Warum sollt' ich mich denn grämen

357.

Es ist gewißlich an der Zeit

362.

O Welt, sieh hier dein Leben

363.

Von Gott will ich nicht lassen

364.

Jesu, meiner Seelen Wonne

365.

O Welt, sieh hier dein Leben

366.

Befiehl du deine Wege

367.

Hilf, Herr Jesu, laß gelingen

368.

Jesu, der du meine Seele

369.

Kommt her zu mir, spricht Gottes Sohn*

370.

Christ lag in Todesbanden

371.

69 Chorale Melodies
with figured bass

Die goldne Sonne, voll Freud' und Wonne

1.

Der lieben Sonnen Licht und Pracht

2.

Der Tag ist hin, die Sonne gehet nieder

3.

Der Tag mit seinem Lichte

4.

Herr, nicht schicke deine Rache

5.

Wo ist mein Schäflein, das ich liebe

6.

94

25. Es ist vollbracht! vergiss ja nicht

26. So giebst du nun, mein Jesu, gute Nacht

27. Auf auf! mein Herz, mit Freuden

28. Jesus, unser Trost und Leben

100

Gott lebet noch

37.

Es kostet viel, ein Christ zu sein

38.

Beglückter Stand getreuer Seelen

39.

104

THE 371 CHORALE HARMONIZATIONS

OWING TO many deficiencies in the way J. S. Bach's chorale harmonizations have been excerpted from larger compositions and published without regard for their context, a very incomplete knowledge of their sources and functions exists among the average student and music-lover. Several things should be definitely clarified concerning these chorale arrangements before a true conception of them can be attained.

1. All of the chorale harmonizations, as far as can be ascertained, were designed to be sung with instrumental support. Even those that appeared in the motets had the support of harpsichord or organ. The three wedding chorales, which were not parts of a larger work, are supported by instruments and instrumental *obbligati*. The singing of these harmonized chorales *a cappella* is based upon a wrong conception, and much of the real character of the harmonization is lost by such a procedure. These sturdy, masculine, vital compositions become suave and effeminate; and hence the true conception is lost when they are sung *a cappella*.

2. They are not congregational hymns. Bach's audiences may have attempted to sing along on the melody in unison, but the harmonizations were never furnished to the congregation. Even in the 69 "Schemelli" songs, only the melody was presented for the congregation. A figured bass was offered for the benefit of the organist who was to vary this with each stanza, adapting his accompaniment to the changing words of each stanza.

3. Modern research has proved that the study of the harmonizations of the Bach chorales is incomplete without considering the words of the text to which the harmonizations were placed. Tonal color and tone-painting were influenced so extensively by the words that sometimes, from a purely musical standpoint, the result is not clear and logical without considering the association of words and music.

4. The early edition of these harmonizations (1784-1787), which is the basis of the present one, was notoriously deficient in many ways, and thereby confused the issue of a correct understanding. Chorales were shortened; instrumental *obbligati*, instrumental parts, and instrumental interludes were omitted by a reduction process which robbed the chorale of its true character.

The most common error in the old edition was a very frequent substitution of the instrumental bass for the vocal bass. Bach always desired his *Continuo*, or instrumental bass, to sound both at the pitch written (*e.g.*, as played by the Violoncello) and an octave lower than written (*i.e.*, as played on the organ pedals and other instruments of 16-foot pitch such as the Contrabass, Bassoon, *etc.*) This lower bass line often corrected the seemingly faulty results caused by the crossing of the bass over the tenor part. It also gave greater dignity to the chorale. In those harmonizations of which the sources still exist in the form of a large work for *soli*, chorus, and orchestra, we find extremely numerous occasions where vocal bass and instrumental bass were interchanged in the early edition of the "371". Another carelessness evident in the early edition resulted from the complete disregard of the words. Ties common to the instrumental parts were carried over into the vocal parts, and the slur-indications were extremely confusing to anyone wishing to fit the words to the music.

In the present edition some of these deficiencies have been rectified in the music, others in the ensuing notes. Within the music the following matters have been corrected:

1. The vocal bass has been given consistently throughout in the same sized notes as the other three voice-parts.

2. The instrumental bass has been given wherever it differs markedly from the vocal bass or wherever it is especially important in showing the harmonic outlines of the setting. When given, the instrumental bass is clearly set off from the vocal bass by being printed in small notes.

3. Other instrumental parts, when similarly important, have been similarly printed. In a

few cases where it was not feasible to present these passages in the music itself, they have been dealt with in the notes.

4. Slurs have been omitted, and the user of the volume is accordingly left free to add slur-indications in terms of the text (original or translation) that he wishes to fit to the music. It should be noted, moreover, that when the words are being fitted to the music many of the remaining ties must be disregarded.

5. Actual wrong notes in the music have been corrected.

In order that this edition of the chorale harmonizations may be made as valuable to the student as possible, the following details have been presented in the notes·

1. The exact words of the stanza or stanzas that accompanied the harmonization in any larger works of Bach which still exist as a source.

2. The key of the harmonization in the source, if its key there is different from that in the "371".

3. A description of the condensation of many chorales.

4. The correct name of the chorale where it has been incorrectly named in the "371".

5. The full indication of the instruments used in the original.

6. Whenever possible, a list of English translations, to assist those whose knowledge of the old German of the cantata texts is limited.

To facilitate reference, the names and numbers of the chorales as they appear in previous editions of the "371" have been retained. Titles of cantatas and the texts of the chorales conform with the Bachgesellschaft edition. In numbering the measures in the remarks under each chorale, partial measures at the beginning are ignored, and the first *complete* measure is considered as the first.

INDEX OF THE 371 CHORALES
ACCORDING TO NUMBER

THIS INDEX is intended for use in connection with the ensuing notes, to bring together the notes on Bach's various harmonizations of the same tune. An index giving the page-number of the music and embracing both the 371 Chorales and the 69 Chorale Melodies will be found on pages xi to xvi.

	Number
Ach bleib bei uns, Herr Jesu Christ	177
Ach Gott, erhör' mein Seufzen	186
Ach Gott und Herr, wie gross und schwer	40, 279
Ach Gott, vom Himmel sieh' darein	3, 253, 262
Ach Gott, wie manches Herzeleid	156, 217, 308
Ach lieben Christen, seid getrost	31, 301
Ach was soll ich Sünder machen	39
Ach wie nichtig, ach wie flüchtig	48
Allein Gott in der Höh' sei Ehr'	125, 249, 313, 326
Allein zu dir, Herr Jesu Christ	13, 359
Alle Menschen müssen sterben	153
Alles ist an Gottes Segen	128
Als der gütige Gott	159
Als Jesus Christus in der Nacht	180
Als vierzig Tag' nach Ostern	208
An Wasserflüssen Babylon	5
Auf, auf, mein Herz, und du mein ganzer Sinn	124
Auf meinen lieben Gott	304
Aus meines Herzens Grunde	1
Aus tiefer Not schrei' ich zu dir	10
Befiehl du deine Wege	270, 286, 340, 367
Christ, der du bist der helle Tag	230
Christe, der du bist Tag und Licht	245
Christe, du Beistand deiner Kreuzgemeine	210
Christ ist erstanden	197
Christ lag in Todesbanden	15, 184, 261, 371
Christum wir sollen loben schon	56
Christ, unser Herr, zum Jordan kam	66, 119
Christus, der ist mein Leben	6, 316
Christus, der uns selig macht	81, 114, 198, 307
Christus ist erstanden, hat überwunden	200
Da der Herr Christ zu Tische sass	196
Danket dem Herren, denn er ist sehr freundlich	228
Dank sei Gott in der Höhe	311
Das alte Jahr vergangen ist	162, 314

	Number
Das neugeborne Kindelein	53, 178
Das walt' Gott Vater und Gott Sohn	224
Das walt' mein Gott	75
Den Vater dort oben	239
Der du bist drei in Einigkeit	154
Der Herr ist mein getreuer Hirt	353
Der Tag, der ist so freudenreich	158
Des heil'gen Geistes reiche Gnad'	207
Die Nacht ist kommen	231
Die Sonn' hat sich mit ihrem Glanz	232
Dies sind die heil'gen zehn Gebot'	127
Dir, dir, Jehovah, will ich singen	209
Du Friedensfürst, Herr Jesu Christ	42
Du grosser Schmerzensmann	167
Du Lebensfürst, Herr Jesu Christ	361
Du, o schönes Weltgebäude	87, 134
Durch Adams Fall ist ganz verderbt	100, 126
Ein' feste Burg ist unser Gott	20, 250, 273
Ein Lämmlein geht und trägt die Schuld	309
Eins ist not! ach Herr, dies Eine	280
Erbarm' dich mein, o Herre Gott	34
Erhalt' uns, Herr, bei deinem Wort	72
Ermuntre dich, mein schwacher Geist	9, 102
Erschienen ist der herrliche Tag	17
Erstanden ist der heil'ge Christ	176
Es ist das Heil uns kommen her	4, 290, 335
Es ist genug; so nimm, Herr	216
Es ist gewisslich an der Zeit	260, 362
Es spricht der Unweisen Mund	27
Es stehn vor Gottes Throne	166
Es wird schier der letzte Tag	238
Es woll' uns Gott genädig sein	16, 333, 352
Freu' dich sehr, o meine Seele	29, 64, 67, 76, 282
Freuet euch, ihr Christen alle	8
Für deinen Thron tret' ich hiermit	334
Für Freuden lasst uns springen	163
Gelobet seist du, Jesu Christ	51, 160, 288
Gib dich zufrieden und sei stille	271

Number

Gott, der du selber bist das Licht........ 225
Gott der Vater wohn' uns bei............. 135
Gott des Himmels und der Erden........ 35
Gottes Sohn ist kommen............... 18
Gott hat das Evangelium............... 181
Gott lebet noch....................... 234
Gottlob, es geht nunmehr zu Ende....... 192
Gott sei gelobet und gebenedeiet........ 70
Gott sei uns gnädig und barmherzig...... 320

Hast du denn, Jesu, dein Angesicht....... 90
Heilig, heilig...................... 235, 319
Helft mir Gott's Güte preisen...... 88, 99, 123
Herr Christ, der ein'ge Gott'ssohn.... 101, 303
Herr Gott, dich loben alle wir........... 164
Herr Gott, dich loben wir............... 205
Herr, ich denk' an jene Zeit............. 212
Herr, ich habe missgehandelt......... 33, 287
Herr Jesu Christ, dich zu uns wend'...... 136
Herr Jesu Christ, du hast bereit......... 226
Herr Jesu Christ, du höchstes Gut 73, 266, 294
Herr Jesu Christ, mein's Lebens Licht..... 295
Herr Jesu Christ, wahr'r Mensch und
   Gott........................... 189, 284
Herr, nun lass in Frieden............... 190
Herr, straf mich nicht in deinem Zorn..... 221
Herr, wie du willst, so schick's mit mir 317, 318
Herzlich lieb hab' ich dich, o Herr........ 277
Herzlich tut mich verlangen............. 21
Herzliebster Jesu, was hast du. 59, 78, 105, 111
Heut' ist, o Mensch, ein grosser......... 168
Heut' triumphieret Gottes Sohn.......... 79
Hilf, Gott, dass mir's gelinge........ 199, 302
Hilf, Herr Jesu, lass gelingen........ 155, 368

Ich bin ja, Herr, in deiner Macht........ 251
Ich dank' dir, Gott, für all' Wohltat....... 223
Ich dank' dir, lieber Herre........ 2, 272, 341
Ich dank' dir schon durch deinen Sohn.... 188
Ich danke dir, o Gott, in deinem Throne... 229
Ich freue mich in dir.................... 60
Ich hab' in Gottes Herz und Sinn........ 349
Ich hab' mein' Sach' Gott heimgestellt.... 19
Ich ruf' zu dir, Herr Jesu Christ.......... 71
Ihr Gestirn', ihr hohlen Lüfte............ 161
In allen meinen Taten........ 50, 140
In dich hab' ich gehoffet, Herr........ 77, 118
In dulci jubilo....................... 143
Ist Gott mein Schild und Helfersmann..... 122

Number

Jesu, deine tiefen Wunden.............. 256
Jesu, der du meine Seele..... 37, 269, 297, **369**
Jesu, der du selbsten wohl.............. 169
Jesu, du mein liebstes Leben............ 116
Jesu, Jesu, du bist mein................ 244
Jesu Leiden, Pein und Tod....... 61, 83, 106
Jesu, meine Freude. 96, 138, 263, 283, 324, 356
Jesu, meiner Seelen Wonne.......... 350, 365
Jesu, meines Herzens Freud'............ 264
Jesu, nun sei gepreiset........... 11, 252, 327
Jesus Christus, unser Heiland........ 30, 174
Jesus, meine Zuversicht.............. 175, 338

Keinen hat Gott verlassen.............. 129
Komm, Gott Schöpfer, heiliger Geist...... 187
Komm, heiliger Geist, Herre Gott........ 69
Kommt her zu mir, spricht Gottes Sohn 45, **370**
Kyrie, Gott Vater in Ewigkeit........... 132

Lass, o Herr, dein Ohr sich neigen....... 218
Liebster Gott, wann werd' ich sterben..... **43**
Liebster Jesu, wir sind hier......... 131, 328
Liebster Immanuel, Herzog der Frommen. 194
Lobet den Herren, denn er ist sehr freundlich 227
Lobt Gott, ihr Christen, allzugleich 54, 276, 342

Mach's mit mir, Gott, nach deiner Güt' 44, 310
Meine Augen schliess' ich jetzt.......... 258
Meinen Jesum lass' ich nicht, Jesus....... 151
Meinen Jesum lass' ich nicht, weil 152, 299, 348
Meine Seele erhebet den Herrn....... 130, 358
Meines Lebens letzte Zeit.............. 346
Mit Fried' und Freud' ich fahr' dahin. 49, 325
Mitten wir im Leben sind............... 214

Nicht so traurig, nicht so sehr........... 149
Nimm von uns, Herr, du treuer Gott...... 292
Nun bitten wir den heiligen Geist.. 36, 84, 97
Nun danket alle Gott............... 32, 330
Nun freut euch, Gottes Kinder all'........ 185
Nun freut euch, lieben Christen, g'mein.. 183
Nun komm, der Heiden Heiland...... 28, 170
Nun lasst uns Gott, dem Herren......... 257
Nun lieget alles unter dir............... 343
Nun lob', mein' Seel', den Herren 7, 116, 268, 296
Nun preiset alle Gottes Barmherzigkeit.... 222
Nun ruhen alle Wälder.. 63, 103, 117, 289, 355
Nun sich der Tag geendet hat........... 240

O Ewigkeit, du Donnerwort.......... 26, 274
O Gott, du frommer Gott.... 85, 312, 315, 337
O grosser Gott von Macht.............. 82

Number

O Haupt voll Blut und Wunden 74, 80, 89, 98, 345
O Herre Gott, dein göttlich Wort........ 14
O Herzensangst, o Bangigkeit........... 173
O Jesu Christ, du höchstes Gut.......... 92
O Jesu, du mein Bräutigam.............. 236
O Lamm Gottes, unschuldig............ 165
O Mensch, bewein' dein' Sünde gross.. 210, 306
O Mensch, schau Jesum Christum an...... 203
O Traurigkeit, o Herzeleid.............. 57
O Welt, sieh hier dein Leben..... 275, 363, 366
O wie selig seid ihr doch, ihr Frommen 213, 219
O wir armen Sünder................... 202

Puer natus in Bethlehem.............. 12

Sanctus, Sanctus Dominus Deus Sabaoth
235, 319
Schaut, ihr Sünder.................... 171
Schmücke dich, o liebe Seele........... 22
Schwing' dich auf zu deinem Gott....... 142
Seelen-Bräutigam..................... 141
Sei gegrüsset, Jesu gütig................. 172
Sei Lob und Ehr' dem höchsten Gut 248, 329, 354
Singen wir aus Herzens Grund.......... 109
Singt dem Herrn ein neues Lied......... 246
So gibst du nun, mein Jesu, gute Nacht... 206
Sollt' ich meinem Gott nicht singen...... 220
Straf' mich nicht in deinem Zorn........ 38

Uns ist ein Kindlein heut' gebor'n........ 148

Valet will ich dir geben.............. 24, 108
Vater unser im Himmelreich...... 47, 110, 267
Verleih' uns Frieden gnädiglich.... 91, 215, 259
Vom Himmel hoch, da komm' ich her... 46, 344
Von Gott will ich nicht lassen 114, 191, 332, 364

Number

Wach' auf, mein Herz, und singe......... 93
Wachet auf, ruft uns die Stimme......... 179
Wär' Gott nicht mit uns diese Zeit... 182, 285
Warum betrübst du dich, mein Herz 94, 145, 300
Warum sollt' ich mich denn grämen... 139, 357
Was betrübst du dich, mein Herze........ 237
Was bist du doch, o Seele, so betrübet.... 193
Was frag' ich nach der Welt......... 255, 291
Was Gott tut, das ist wohlgetan.. 65, 293, 347
Was mein Gott will, das g'scheh' 41, 115, 120, 265
Was willst du dich, o meine Seele........ 241
Weg, mein Herz, mit den Gedanken... 254, 298
Welt, ade! ich bin dein müde............ 150
Weltlich Ehr' und zeitlich Gut........... 211
Wenn ich in Angst und Not............. 147
Wenn mein Stündlein vorhanden ist 52, 322, 351
Wenn wir in höchsten Nöten sein..... 68, 247
Werde munter, mein Gemüte..... 95, 121, 233
Wer Gott vertraut, hat wohl gebaut....... 137
Wer in dem Schutz des Höchsten ist....... 144
Wer nur den lieben Gott lässt
62, 104, 112, 146, 339
Wer weiss, wie nahe mir mein Ende....... 204
Wie bist du, Seele, in mir so gar betrübt... 242
Wie schön leuchtet der Morgenstern
86, 195, 278, 305, 323
Wir Christenleut'................. 55, 321, 360
Wir glauben all' an einen Gott, Schöpfer... 133
Wo Gott der Herr nicht bei uns hält...... 336
Wo Gott zum Haus nicht gibt sein' Gunst. 157
Wo soll ich fliehen hin........... 25, 281, 331

Zeuch ein zu deinen Toren.............. 23

ABBREVIATIONS USED IN THE ENSUING NOTES

Bachgesellschaft W   Franz Wüllner, ed.: *Choräle für vier Singstimmen aus der Sammlung von C. P. E. Bach*, in *Joh. Seb. Bach's Motetten, Choräle und Lieder*, in the Bachgesellschaft ed. of Bach's works, Bd. XXXIX (Breitkopf und Härtel, Leipzig, 1892), pp. 177-276.

Erk   Ludwig Erk, ed.: *Johann Sebastian Bach's mehrstimmige Choralgesänge und geistliche Arien* (C. F. Peters, Leipzig, 1850-1865).

Richter   B. Fr. Richter, ed.: *389 Choralgesänge* (Breitkopf und Härtel, Leipzig, n. d.)

Schirmer B-R   Charles N. Boyd and Albert Riemenschneider, eds.: *Chorales by Johann Sebastian Bach* (G. Schirmer, Inc., New York, 1939-   ).

Smend   Friedrich Smend, rev.: *Johann Sebastian Bach: Mehrstimmige Choräle. . . herausgegeben von Ludwig Erk* (C. F. Peters, Leipzig, 1932).

Terry   Charles Sanford Terry, ed.: *The Four-Part Chorals of J. S. Bach* (Oxford University Press, London, 1929).

NOTES ON THE 371 CHORALES

SOMEWHAT LESS than one half of these chorales were taken from larger works which were lost after they had been copied for the manuscript collection which formed the basis of this edition. Because no known sources exist for these, no attempt has been made to supply either a text or the orchestration. From a study of those for which the sources are available, it is a comparatively simple deduction to state that all chorales were originally supplied with instrumental support. Through an exhaustive study of the tone-painting and aesthetics of Bach applied to the chorales, in much the same manner as the methods employed by Pirro in his *L'Esthétique de J. S. Bach*, it might be possible to supply many of the missing stanzas of the hymns to these chorales. In the ensuing notes, the symbol (n.s.) after the chorale-name means that no source is known for the particular harmonization.

1. Aus meines Herzens Grunde (n.s.)

2. Ich dank' dir, lieber Herre (n.s.)

3. Ach Gott, vom Himmel sieh' darein

From Cantata 153, "Schau', lieber Gott, wie meine Feind'". This is a solo cantata for alto, tenor, and bass, but contains three chorales, of which the present number opens the cantata, the other two appear at the middle and at the end of the work.

In addition to the four voice parts, this chorale is scored for *Violino I* with the soprano, *Violino II* with the alto, *Viola* with the tenor, and the *Continuo* with the bass part.

The text of the stanza that Bach here used (the first stanza in the hymn) is as follows:

> *Schau', lieber Gott, wie meine Feind',*
> *damit ich stets muss kämpfen,*
> *so listig und so mächtig seind,*
> *dass sie mich leichtlich dämpfen!*
> *Herr, wo mich deine Gnad' nicht hält,*
> *so kann der Teufel, Fleisch und Welt*
> *mich leicht in Unglück stürzen.*

Terry, no. 8, presents this stanza along with the fifth and seventh stanzas of the hymn, and his own English translations. He presents the last line of the first stanza incorrectly, so far as Bach's use of it is concerned, by giving the reading: *Das Fleisch geschwind verführen*. Dr. Charles N. Boyd made a very good translation of the correct German text for the first stanza and pub-lished it in the close-score division of Schirmer B-R, book I, p. 78.

Note the crossing of voices on the last beat of measure 6 and the first beat of measure 7. There is also a discrepancy here between the reading of the autograph score and the original parts, which are not autograph.

4. Es ist das Heil uns kommen her

From Cantata 86, "Wahrlich, ich sage euch". This is a solo cantata for soprano, alto, tenor, and bass, in which this number is placed as the concluding chorale.

The instrumentation for this cantata, as indicated in the Bachgesellschaft edition, is for strings and two oboes; but their distribution in this chorale is not indicated.

The text that Bach used was the eleventh stanza of the hymn.

> *Die Hoffnung wart't der rechten Zeit,*
> *was Gottes Wort zusaget:*
> *wenn das geschehen soll zur Freud',*
> *setzt Gott kein' g'wisse Tage.*
> *Er weiss wohl, wenn's am besten ist,*
> *und braucht an uns kein' arge List,*
> *dess soll'n wir ihm vertrauen.*

In addition, Terry, no. 89, presents the first and twelfth stanzas, together with his own English translations.

5. An Wasserflüssen Babylon (n.s.)

This chorale appears here in the key of G. As No. 309 of the "371" it appears under the title "Ein Lämmlein geht und trägt die Schuld"' in the key of A♭. The only difference lies in the alto and tenor parts of the third measure from the end, which are presented in a slightly different reading. In No. 309, a somewhat different manner of writing is used in presenting a few of the notes. Both Erk, no. 161, and Smend, no. 22, present only the A♭ version, with the words "Ein Lämmlein geht und trägt die Schuld". Bachgesellschaft W, no. 15, presents only the G major version, with the first stanza of both hymns. Richter does the same. Terry, no. 24, also follows Bachgesellschaft W, but presents two stanzas from each hymn, with translations.

6. Christus, der ist mein Leben (n.s.)

7. Nun lob', mein' Seel', den Herren

From Cantata 17, "Wer Dank opfert, der preiset mich", where it is found as the closing number of the second part. It there has the words of the third stanza of the hymn.

> *Wie sich ein Vat'r erbarmet*
> *üb'r seine junge Kindlein klein:*
> *so thut der Herr uns Armen,*
> *so wir ihn kindlich fürchten rein.*
> *Er kennt das arm' Gemächte,*
> *er weiss, wir sind nur Staub.*
> *Gleich wie das Gras vom Reche,*
> *ein' Blum' und fallend Laub—*
> *der Wind nur drüber wehet,*
> *so ist es nimmer da:*
> *also der Mensch vergehet,*
> *sein End', das ist ihm nah.*

The text did not appear in the autograph score. Erk, no. 101, printed the first stanza of the hymn as the appropriate one for this setting. The discovery later of the orchestra parts in which the third stanza was indicated as the proper one proved that he was wrong in his deduction. Smend, no. 211, corrects the error in his revised edition. Terry, no. 276, presents stanzas I and III, with English translations. Catherine Winkworth's translation, made for the *Chorale Book for England* (1863), is found in Schirmer B-R, book I, p. 102 f.

The orchestration is in motet style, the instrument parts agreeing entirely with the voice

parts: *Oboi I & II* and *Violino I* with the soprano, *Violino II* with the alto, *Viola* with the tenor, and *Continuo* with the bass.

Another harmonization of the same chorale, in ¾ meter, appears among the "371" as No. 268.

8. Freuet euch, ihr Christen

Taken from Cantata 40, "Dazu ist erschienen der Sohn Gottes". This cantata contains three chorales, of which this one closes the work. The other two appear as Nos. 321 and 142 of the "371". The words used with the chorale in the present harmonization are the fourth stanza of the hymn.

> *Jesu, nimm dich deiner Glieder*
> *ferner in Genaden an;*
> *schenke, was man bitten kann,*
> *zu erquicken deine Brüder:*
> *gieb der ganzen Christenschaar*
> *Frieden und ein sel'ges Jahr!*
> *Freude, Freude über Freude!*
> *Christus wehret allem Leide.*
> *Wonne, Wonne über Wonne!*
> *er ist die Genadensonne.*

Terry, no. 110, presents two further stanzas, I and III, as well as the English translations for them by Catherine Winkworth. Schirmer B-R, book I, 112, also uses the Winkworth translation.

The orchestration is in motet style, as follows: with the soprano, *Corno I, Oboe I,* and *Violino I;* with the alto, *Oboe II* and *Violino II;* with the tenor, *Viola;* and, with the bass, the *Continuo.*

9. Ermuntre dich, mein schwacher Geist

From the "Christmas Oratorio", where it is placed as the third number of Part II. It there has the text of the ninth stanza of the hymn.

> *Brich an, o schönes Morgenlicht,*
> *und lass den Himmel tagen!*
> *Du Hirtenvolk, erschrecke nicht,*
> *weil dir die Engel sagen:*
> *dass dieses schwache Knäbelein*
> *soll unser Trost und Freude sein,*
> *dazu den Satan zwingen*
> *und letztlich Frieden bringen.*

Terry also prints the first, third, and twelfth stanzas, with his own English translations. In Schirmer B-R, book I, p. 95, appears an English translation by the author of these notes.

The instruments coincide with the voices in motet style, thus: soprano, *Flauti traversi I & II* (*in 8va*), *Oboi d'amore I & II*, and *Violino I;* alto, *Oboe da caccia I* and *Violino II;* tenor, *Oboe da caccia II* and *Viola;* and bass, *Organo* and *Continuo*. In the last measure the *Oboe da caccia* differs from the tenor part; and Terry, no. 84, has accordingly been led to add a C on the last half of the second beat in the tenor.

10. Aus tiefer Not schrei' ich zu dir

From Cantata 38, "Aus tiefer Noth", where it has its place as the closing chorale of the work. It there appears with stanza V:

> *Ob bei uns ist der Sünden viel,*
> *bei Gott ist viel mehr Gnade,*
> *sein' Hand zu helfen hat kein Ziel,*
> *wie gross auch sei der Schade.*
> *Er ist allein der gute Hirt,*
> *der Israel erlösen wird*
> *aus seinen Sünden allen.*

Terry, no. 32, prints stanzas I and II in addition to stanza V. For these stanzas he also gives English translations by George Macdonald. Schirmer B-R, book I, p. 79, uses a translation of stanza V by Arthur Tozer Russell.

The instrumentation is again in motet form: *Oboi I & II*, *Violino I*, and *Trombone I* play with the soprano; *Violino II* and *Trombone II*, with the alto; *Viola* and *Trombone III*, with the tenor; and *Trombone IV* and *Continuo*, with the bass.

11. Jesu, nun sei gepreiset

From Cantata 41, "Jesu, nun sei gepreiset", where it is used as the concluding number. It there has the text of the third stanza:

> *Dein ist allein die Ehre,*
> *dein ist allein der Ruhm;*
> *Geduld im Kreuz uns lehre,*
> *regier' all' unser Thun,*
> *bis wir fröhlich abscheiden*
> *in's ewig' Himmelreich,*
> *zu wahren Fried' und Freude,*

> *den Heil'gen Gottes gleich.*
> *Indess mach's mit uns Allen*
> *nach deinem Wohlgefallen:*
> *solch's singet heut ohn' Scherzen*
> *die Christgläubige Schaar,*
> *und wünscht mit Mund und Herzen*
> *ein selig's neues Jahr,*
> *und wünscht mit Mund und Herzen*
> *ein selig's neues Jahr.*

Terry, no. 217, presents his own translation. Schirmer B-R, book II, no. 101, offers a translation by Dr. Charles N. Boyd.

In the full score, *Oboi I*, *II*, and *III* are written out on separate staves, but largely duplicate the soprano, alto, and tenor voice-parts, respectively; similarly *Violini I & II* and *Viola*, on separate staves, duplicate soprano, alto, and tenor. The *Organo* and *Continuo* duplicate the bass part. The fourth, the eighth, and the last measures in this reduction of the chorale represent, each, two measures in the original. At each of these three places a two-measure fanfare for two trumpets and kettledrums entered on the long notes. The joyous, festal character of the original form has been partly lost in the present abbreviated version.

In almost identical form (but in the key of D) and with the same text, this chorale was used as the closing number in Cantata 171, "Gott, wie dein Name, so ist auch dein Ruhm". There the *Oboi*, *Violini*, and *Viola* parts are merely indicated as following the voice parts, but the Trumpet and Timpani parts are written out on separate staves. Several of the *Continuo* notes there show changes, but otherwise the harmonization is the same.

12. Puer natus in Bethlehem

From Cantata 65, "Sie werden aus Saba Alle kommen", where it is placed as the second number of the work, with the words:

> *Die Kön'ge aus Saba kamen dar, kamen dar,*
> *Gold, Weihrauch, Myrrhen brachten sie dar,*
> *Alleluja! Alleluja!*

Flauto I and *Flauto II* are indicated on a separate staff, agreeing with the soprano part but written one octave higher. *Oboe da caccia I* and *Oboe da caccia II* are also written on separate staves, but agree with the alto and tenor respectively. It may be assumed that the Strings duplicated the voice parts. H. M. MacGill, in *Songs of the Christian Creed* (London: 1876), presents an English translation, which is used in Schirmer B-R, book I, p. 89.

13. Allein zu dir, Herr Jesu Christ

From Cantata 33, "Allein zu dir, Herr Jesu Christ", where it is presented as the closing number. The text is the fourth stanza of the hymn.

> *Ehr' sei Gott in dem höchsten Thron,*
> *dem Vater aller Güte,*
> *und Jesum Christ, sein'm liebsten Sohn,*
> *der uns allzeit behüte,*
> *und Gott, dem heiligen Geiste,*
> *der uns sein' Hülf' allzeit leiste,*
> *damit wir ihm gefällig sein,*
> *hier in dieser Zeit*
> *und folgends in der Ewigkeit.*

Terry, no. 18, presents in addition the first two stanzas of the hymn, and his own English translations. Catherine Winkworth, in her *Lyra Germanica* (1858), also has a translation which was later revised for the *Chorale Book for England*. The latter form of her translation is used in Schirmer B-R, book I, p. 109.

Oboe I and *Violino I* play with the soprano; *Oboe II* and *Violino II*, with the alto; *Viola,* with the tenor; and *Organo* and *Continuo*, with the bass.

14. O Herre Gott, dein göttlich Wort (n.s.)

In Cantata 184, "Erwünschtes Freudenlicht", there is a somewhat similar harmonization of this melody, in the key of D, not included among the "371". Erk, p. iii, regards the present form as a transposition of the cantata version. His assumption is not borne out, however, by a detailed comparison of the two versions.

15. Christ lag in Todesbanden (n.s.)

There are three other harmonizations of the same chorale in this volume: Nos. 184, 261, and 371

16. Es woll' uns Gott genädig sein (n.s.)

Two other harmonizations of this chorale exist in this collection: Nos. 333 and 352.

17. Erschienen ist der herrliche Tag

From Cantata 145, "So du mit deinem Munde bekennest Jesum", where it is placed as the closing number with the words of the fourteenth stanza:

> *Drum wir auch billig fröhlich sein,*
> *singen das Halleluja fein,*
> *und loben dich, Herr Jesu Christ;*
> *zu Trost du uns erstanden bist.*
> *Halleluja!*

Terry, no. 87, presents stanzas I, X, XII, XIII, and XIV, with his own translations.

The instrumentation for the chorale is not specifically designated, but that for the cantata is as follows: *Tromba, Flauto traverso, Oboi d'amore I & II*, and Strings.

Erk's contention that the writer of the manuscript upon which the present collection is based deliberately transposed some of the chorales from their original keys seems to be substantiated here. In the cantata, this chorale begins and ends on F♯, with two sharps in the signature giving a decided Phrygian flavor to the composition. In the "371" it appears transposed down one step with the signature of one sharp. Both Terry and Richter present the original key of the cantata but use the signature of four sharps to simplify the notation. This is a doubtful procedure, as it tends to obscure the mode.

18. Gottes Sohn ist kommen (n.s.)

19. Ich hab' mein' Sach' Gott heimgestellt (n.s.)

20. Ein' feste Burg ist unser Gott (n.s.)

This chorale appears harmonized two other times in this collection: as No. 250, which—like the present number—is from a lost larger composition, and as No. 273, which is from Cantata 80. All three versions are strong harmonizations of a sterling Reformation chorale.

21. Herzlich tut mich verlangen

This chorale was evidently a great favorite of Bach's, for he has left eleven harmonizations of it, five of which are found in the "St. Matthew Passion". This particular harmonization is from Cantata 153, "Schau', lieber Gott, wie meine Feind'", where it occupies a middle position in the cantata. Other chorales are used at the beginning and at the end of the work. The words of the text are the fifth stanza:

> *Und obgleich alle Teufel*
> *dir wollten widerstehn,*
> *so wird doch ohne Zweifel*
> *Gott nicht zurücke gehn;*
> *was er ihm fürgenommen*
> *und was er haben will,*
> *das muss doch endlich kommen*
> *zu seinem Zweck und Ziel.*

Terry, no. 163, presents stanzas I, V, and VI, with his own English translations.

Violino I plays with the soprano; *Violino II*, with the alto; *Viola*, with the tenor; and *Continuo*, with the bass.

Other harmonizations of this chorale among the "371" are as follows: under the name "Befiehl du deine Wege", Nos. 270, 286, and 367 (No. 340 under the same name is a different melody); and, under the name "O Haupt voll Blut und Wunden", Nos. 74, 80, 89, 98, and 345.

22. Schmücke dich, o liebe Seele

From Cantata 180, "Schmücke dich, o liebe Seele", where it is the closing number of the cantata. It there has the ninth stanza as the text:

> *Jesu, wahres Brod des Lebens,*
> *hilf, dass ich doch nicht vergebens,*
> *oder mir vielleicht zum Schaden*
> *sei zu deinem Tisch geladen.*
> *Lass mich durch dies Seelen-Essen*
> *deine Liebe recht ermessen,*
> *dass ich auch, wie jetzt auf Erden,*
> *mög' ein Gast im Himmel werden.*

Terry, no. 314, presents stanzas I, II, IV, and IX, with his own English translations. Catherine Winkworth, in *Lyra Germanica* (1858), also has a good translation, which is to be found on page 124 of Book I, Schirmer B-R.

This is one of the chorales that have been transposed from their original key. In the cantata the key is F major, while in the "371" it appears in E♭ major.

The instrumentation for the cantata is *Flauti I & II*, *Oboi I & II* (*Oboe da caccia*), Strings, and *Continuo*. There are no special indications for the distribution of the instruments in the chorale, but we may assume that the customary use was made of them with the voice-parts.

23. Zeuch ein zu deinen Toren

The name of this chorale should be "Helft mir Gott's Güte preisen"; it is simply a duplication of No. 88, which is listed under its correct name. It is the last movement of Cantata 28, "Gottlob! nun geht das Jahr zu Ende", with the sixth stanza of the hymn.

> *All' solch' dein' Güt' wir preisen,*
> *Vater in's Himmelsthron,*
> *die du uns thust beweisen,*
> *durch Christum, deinen Sohn,*
> *und bitten ferner dich:*
> *gieb uns ein friedlich's Jahre,*
> *für allem Leid bewahre*
> *und nähr' uns mildiglich.*

Terry, no. 128, offers a translation from John Christian Jacobi's *Psalmodia Germanica*.

Oboe I, *Violino I*, and *Cornetto* play with the soprano; *Oboe II*, *Violino II*, and *Trombone*, with the alto; *Taille*, *Viola*, and *Trombone II*, with the tenor; and *Continuo* and *Trombone III*, with the bass.

24. Valet will ich dir geben (n.s)

It is probable that the low D in the second measure and the last bass note of the chorale—possibly the whole last phrase—were originally an octave higher in the vocal bass. Another harmonization may be found as No. 108.

25. Wo soll ich fliehen hin

This melody is commonly known as "Auf meinen lieben Gott", and should have been so named here. When Bach referred to the melody "Wo soll ich fliehen hin", he had in mind a tune different from the one here harmonized. For example, in Cantata 163, Bach closes the work by presenting only a figured bass to the chorale, "Wo soll ich fliehen hin", marked as follows: "Choral. In simplice stylo." Terry, no. 487, gives this with the correct melody. But it is a different melody from the one here under consideration.

The present chorale is another example of transposition from the original. It appears in Cantata 148, "Bringet dem Herrn Ehre seines Namens", as the last number, with the signature of F♯ minor. The change to F minor with only three flats that was effected when this chorale was placed among the "371" lends a Dorian characteristic to its signature.

The only existing copy of the score, Gottlob Harrer's manuscript, does not indicate the words of the chorale. Spitta's researches have designated the eleventh stanza:

> *Führ' auch mein Herz und Sinn*
> *durch deinen Geist dahin,*
> *dass ich mög' alles meiden,*
> *was mich und dich kann scheiden,*
> *und ich an deinem Leibe*
> *ein Gliedmass ewig bleibe.*

Terry, no. 26, presents an anonymous translation from the *Moravian Hymn-book* (1754).

The instrumentation of the cantata is for *Tromba, Oboi I, II, & III,* Strings, and *Continuo.* No designation of the distribution of these instruments in the chorale is given.

26. O Ewigkeit, du Donnerwort

From Cantata 20, "O Ewigkeit, du Donnerwort", where it appears twice—once in the middle portion of the work and again at the close. The first time, the text is the eleventh stanza of the hymn; and the second time it is the sixteenth.

> 11. *So lang ein Gott im Himmel lebt*
>   *und über alle Wolken schwebt,*
>   *wird solche Marter währen:*
>   *es wird sie plagen Kält' und Hitz',*
>   *Angst, Hunger, Schrecken, Feu'r und Blitz*
>   *und sie doch nicht verzehren.*
>   *Denn wird sich enden diese Pein,*
>   *wenn Gott nicht mehr wird ewig sein.*

> 16. *O Ewigkeit, du Donnerwort,*
>   *o Schwert, das durch die Seele bohrt,*

> *o Anfang sonder Ende!*
> *O Ewigkeit, Zeit ohne Zeit,*
> *ich weiss vor grosser Traurigkeit*
> *nicht, wo ich mich hin wende.*
> *Nimm du mich, wenn es dir gefällt,*
> *Herr Jesu, in dein Freudenzelt.*

Schirmer B-R, I, p. 88, uses a translation of the sixteenth stanza by J. C. Jacobi. Terry, no. 283, presents his own translations for the first, eleventh, and sixteenth stanzas.

Tromba da tirarsi, Oboi I & II, and *Violino I* play with the soprano; *Oboe III* and *Violino II,* with the alto; *Viola,* with the tenor; and *Continuo,* with the bass.

27. Es spricht der Unweisen Mund (n.s.)

It is possible that the low bass F in the sixth measure was an octave higher in the voice part.

28. Nun komm, der Heiden Heiland

This is the closing number of Cantata 36, "Schwingt freudig euch empor". The text consists of the eighth stanza:

> *Lob sei Gott dem Vater g'thon,*
> *Lob sei Gott sein'm ein'gen Sohn,*
> *Lob sei Gott dem heil'gen Geist*
> *immer und in Ewigkeit!*

Schirmer B-R, I, p. 88, presents a translation by the author of these notes. Terry, no. 271, presents his own translations of stanzas 1, 2, 3, 4, and 8.

Oboe d'amore I and *Violino I* play with the soprano; *Oboe d'amore II* and *Violino II,* with the alto; *Viola,* with the tenor; and *Organo* and *Continuo,* with the bass.

29. Freu' dich sehr, o meine Seele

This chorale is from Cantata 32, "Liebster Jesu, mein Verlangen", where it brings the work to a close with the twelfth stanza of the hymn.

> *Mein Gott, öffne mir die Pforten*
> *solcher Gnad' und Gütigkeit,*
> *lass mich allzeit aller Orten*
> *schmecken deine Süssigkeit!*
> *Liebe mich, und treib' mich an,*
> *dass ich dich, so gut ich kann,*
> *wiederum umfang' und liebe,*
> *und ja nun nicht mehr betrübe.*

Schirmer B-R, I, p. 82, offers a translation by Dr. Charles N. Boyd. Terry, no. 103, offers his own translation.

Oboe and *Violino I* agree with the soprano, except for one small passing note in the Oboe part; *Violino II* agrees with the alto; and *Viola* agrees with the tenor. In the full score these instrumental parts, as well as the *Continuo*, are written on separate staves.

30. Jesus Christus, unser Heiland (n.s.)

There are two melodies known under this name. The other one is found as No. 174 of this collection. It is probable that the low E in the bass of measure 3 and the same note in the final measure should be an octave higher for the vocal bass.

31. Ach lieben Christen, seid getrost (n. s.)

Another harmonization, under the same title, is found as No. 301. But the more common name by which this chorale was known is "Wo Gott der Herr nicht bei uns hält", and as such it is listed in the harmonization which is No. 336 in the present volume.

32. Nun danket alle Gott (n.s.)

One of the best-known of the chorales. Another harmonization is found as No. 330. The low E of the next-to-last note in the bass was probably taken from the instrumental part.

33. Herr, ich habe missgehandelt (n.s.)

Another harmonization of the same tune is found as No. 287.

34. Erbarm' dich mein, o Herre Gott (n.s.)

There can be little doubt that the extreme low notes, especially in the next-to-last measure, were incorrectly copied from the instrumental bass. An interesting composition based upon this chorale melody is the short organ prelude of the same name.

35. Gott des Himmels und der Erden

Found in the "Christmas Oratorio", where it appears with the ninth stanza of the hymn and brings the fifth section of the oratorio to a close.

Zwar ist solche Herzensstube
wohl kein schöner Fürstensaal,
sondern eine finstre Grube;
doch, sobald dein Gnadenstrahl
in dieselbe nur wird blinken,
wird sie voller Sonnen dünken.

An English translation by the author of these notes is found in Book I of Schirmer B-R, p. 97. Terry, no. 119, also offers his own translation.

Oboi d'amore I & II and *Violino I* play with the soprano; *Violino II*, with the alto; *Viola*, with the tenor; and *Organo* and *Continuo*, with the bass.

36. Nun bitten wir den heiligen Geist (n.s.)

Two other harmonizations of the same melody are found as Nos. 84 and 97.

37. Jesu, der du meine Seele (n.s)

Nos. 269, 297, and 369 are harmonizations of the same melody.

38. Straf' mich nicht in deinem Zorn

This chorale is from Cantata 115, "Mache dich, mein Geist, bereit", where it appears as the closing number, with the text of the tenth stanza:

Drum so lasst uns immerdar
wachen, flehen, beten,
weil die Angst, Noth und Gefahr
immer näher treten;
denn die Zeit
ist nicht weit,
da uns Gott wird richten,
und die Welt vernichten.

Schirmer B-R, book I, p. 105, presents an English translation by Dr. Emanuel Cronenwett. Terry, no. 323, presents his own translation.

The instrumentation is as follows: *Corno, Flauto, Oboe d'amore,* and *Violino I* with the soprano; *Violino II* with the alto; *Viola* with the tenor; and *Continuo* with the bass.

This is one of the chorales that, in the preparation of the "371", suffered transposition. The key is here Eb major, while in the cantata it is G major. Another slight difference between the two versions exists: in the last measure of the cantata version, the tenor is slightly more ornate, with the following reading:

39.   Ach was soll ich Sünder machen (n.s.)

This no doubt had its origin in one of the lost cantatas.   The low bass notes in measures 6, 7, and 12 were probably taken from the instrumental bass part.

40.   Ach Gott und Herr (n.s.)

Number 279 of this edition presents the harmonization from Cantata 48.

41.   Was mein Gott will, das

Like No. 12, this is from Cantata 65, "Sie werden aus Saba alle kommen".   There it closes the work with a setting of the tenth stanza:

> *Ei nun, mein Gott, so fall' ich dir*
> *getrost in deine Hände,*
> *nimm mich, und mach' es so mit mir*
> *bis an mein letztes Ende:*
> *wie du wohl weisst,*
> *dass meinem Geist*
> *dadurch sein Weg entstehe,*
> *und deine Ehr'*
> *je mehr und mehr*
> *sich in mir selbst erhöhe.*

Terry, no. 359, offers his own translation.
The instrumentation is not specifically designated for the chorale in the full score, but is no doubt the same as for the cantata as a whole, for which the instruments are *Corni I & II, Flauti I & II, Oboi da caccia I & II*, Strings, and *Continuo*.

42.   Du Friedensfürst, Herr Jesu Christ

This chorale closes Cantata 67, "Halt' im Gedächtniss Jesum Christ", with the first stanza of the hymn.

> *Du Friedefürst, Herr Jesu Christ,*
> *wahr'r Mensch und wahrer Gott,*
> *ein starker Nothhelfer du bist*
> *im Leben und im Tod:*

> *drum wir allein*
> *im Namen dein*
> *zu deinem Vater schreien.*

Schirmer B-R, book I, p. 80, presents an English translation by J. C. Jacobi.
Corno da tirarsi, Flauto traverso, Oboe d'amore I, and *Violino I* are indicated to play with the soprano; *Oboe d'amore II* and *Violino II*, with the alto; *Viola*, with the tenor; and *Organo* and *Continuo*, with the bass.

43.   Liebster Gott, wann werd' ich sterben

The origin of this chorale is Cantata 8, "Liebster Gott, wann werd' ich sterben", where it appears as the closing number with the text of the fifth stanza:

> *Herrscher über Tod und Leben,*
> *mach' einmal mein Ende gut,*
> *lehre mich den Geist aufgeben*
> *mit recht wohlgefasstem Muth.*
> *Hilf, dass ich ein ehrlich Grab*
> *neben frommen Christen hab'*
> *und auch endlich in der Erde*
> *nimmermehr zu Schanden werde.*

In Schirmer B-R, book I, p. 122, a translation by the author of these notes will be found. Terry, no. 233, also presents his own translation.
In the full score, *Violino I, Flauto traverso (in 8va), Oboe d'amore I,* and *Corno* play the soprano part; *Violino II* and *Oboe d'amore II*, the alto; *Viola*, the tenor; and *Continuo*, the bass.

44.   Mach's mit mir, Gott, nach deiner Güt' (n.s.)

This harmonization is from one of the lost cantatas.   Terry gives stanzas 1, 2, and 5 of the hymn with his own translations. Another harmonization of the melody may be found as No. 310 of the present edition.

45.   Kommt her zu mir, spricht

This is the final number of Cantata 108, "Es ist euch gut, dass ich hingehe", where it has the following stanza as its text:

> *Dein Geist, den Gott vom Himmel giebt,*
> *der leitet Alles, was ihn liebt,*
> *auf wohl gebahnten Wegen.*

Er setzt und richtet unsern Fuss,
dass er nicht anders treten muss,
als wo man find't den Segen.

Oboi d'amore I & II and *Violino I* play with the soprano; *Violino II*, with the alto; *Viola*, with the tenor; and *Continuo*, with the bass.

46. Vom Himmel hoch, da komm' ich her

This chorale brings to a close the first part of the "Christmas Oratorio". As originally laid out in the Oratorio, each verse-line is separated by a fanfare two measures in length, played by three trumpets and by kettledrums. The omission of this instrumental part in the "371" has caused the second and fourth verse-lines of this chorale to be introduced upon the fourth beat instead of the second, thereby causing a slight shifting of the accent.

Flauti traversi I & II (in 8va), *Oboi I & II*, and *Violino I* play with the soprano; *Violino II*, with the alto; *Viola*, with the tenor; and *Fagotto, Organo*, and *Continuo*, with the bass.

The words are those of the thirteenth stanza:

Ach, mein herzliebes Jesulein!
mach' dir ein rein sanft Bettelein,
zu ruh'n in meines Herzens Schrein,
dass ich nimmer vergesse dein.

Terry, no. 335, offers the translation by Catherine Winkworth from the *Chorale Book for England* (1865).

47. Vater unser im Himmelreich

The inclusion of this chorale in this set would indicate that the copyist used the first or second version of the "St. John Passion" for his source, rather than the third and final revision. The present chorale differs from the form found in the first two versions of the "St. John Passion" in only two small details. To make the chorale as given here conform with that in the "St. John Passion" (first and second version), the second note of the tenor in the fifth full measure should be omitted and the low F of the bass in the tenth measure should be placed an octave higher.

The words are those of the fourth stanza:

Dein Will' gescheh', Herr Gott, zugleich
auf Erden wie im Himmelreich;

gieb uns Geduld in Leidenszeit,
Gehorsamsein in Lieb' und Leid,
wehr' und steur' allem Fleisch und Blut,
das wider deinen Willen thut.

Terry, no. 327, offers the English translation by George Macdonald; Schirmer B-R, book I, p. 106, that by Catherine Winkworth.

Flauti traversi I & II, *Oboi I & II*, and *Violino I* play with the soprano; *Violino II*, with the alto; *Viola*, with the tenor; and *Organo* and *Continuo*, with the bass.

There are two other versions of this chorale in this collection: Nos. 110 and 267.

48. Ach wie nichtig, ach wie flüchtig

From Cantata 26, "Ach wie flüchtig, ach wie nichtig", where, with the text of the thirteenth stanza, it appears as the closing number.

Ach wie flüchtig, ach wie nichtig
sind der Menschen Sachen!
Alles, Alles, was wir sehen,
das muss fallen und vergehen;
wer Gott fürcht't, bleibt ewig stehen.

Both Schirmer B-R, I, p. 92, and Terry, no. 12, offer the English translation by Sir John Bowring. Attention is called to the changed position of "*nichtig*" and "*flüchtig*" in the title of this chorale as it appears in the "371".

Corno, Flauto traverso, Oboi I & II, and *Violino I* play with the soprano; *Oboe III* and *Violino II*, with the alto; *Viola*, with the tenor; and *Organo* and *Continuo*, with the bass.

49. Mit Fried' und Freud' ich fahr' dahin (n.s.)

From one of the lost cantatas. The last bass note was evidently copied from the instrumental bass.

50. In allen meinen Taten

This chorale is here incorrectly named. The usual tune known under this name is found as No. 140 of this set. The correct name for No. 50 is "O Welt, ich muss dich lassen". Sometimes it is also known as "Nun ruhen alle Wälder". The present harmonization is taken from the "St. Matthew Passion", where it appears with the third stanza of the hymn.

Wer hat dich so geschlagen,
mein Heil, und dich mit Plagen
so übel zugericht?
Du bist ja nicht ein Sünder,
wie wir und unsre Kinder;
von Missethaten weisst du nicht.

Terry, no. 300, offers his own translation. Schirmer B-R, I, p. 104, presents the John S. Dwight translation.

Flauti traversi I & II, Oboi I & II, and *Violino I* play the soprano part; *Violino II,* the alto; *Viola,* the tenor; and *Organo* and *Continuo,* the bass.

51. Gelobet seist du, Jesu Christ

This chorale appears as the closing number of Cantata 91, "Gelobet seist du, Jesu Christ". The stanza of the hymn is the seventh:

Das hat er Alles uns gethan,
sein' gross' Lieb' zu zeigen an;
dess freu' sich alle Christenheit,
und dank' ihm dess in Ewigkeit.
Kyrieleis!

Terry, no 113, presents his own English translation. Schirmer B-R, I, p. 82, uses one by Richard Massie.

In the score, *Corno I, Corno II,* and *Timpani* appear on separate staves, with more or less independent parts. In addition, *Oboi I, II, & III* and *Violino I* play with the soprano; *Violino II,* with the alto; *Viola,* with the tenor; and *Continuo,* with the bass. The low C in the last measure is the actual vocal bass as presented in the full score.

In the Bachgesellschaft edition, vol. XVI, p. 371, this chorale appears in simple form as a variant to one in Cantata 64. It has there the same stanza of the text as is given above.

52. Wenn mein Stündlein vorhanden ist
(n.s.)

Other harmonizations are found as Nos. 322 and 351.

53. Das neugeborne Kindelein

This is a duplicate of the harmonization found under No. 178. It is from Cantata 122, "Das neugebor'ne Kindelein", where it brings the work to a close with the fourth stanza:

Es bringt das rechte Jubeljahr,
was trauern wir denn immerdar?
Frisch auf! itzt ist es Singenszeit,
das Jesulein wend't alles Leid.

Schirmer B-R, I, p. 93, uses an anonymous translation from *The Ohio Lutheran Hymnal* (1880); Terry, no. 60, presents his own translation.

The instrumentation is as follows: *Oboe I* and *Violino I* with soprano, *Oboe II* and *Violino II* with alto, *Taille* and *Viola* with tenor, and *Continuo* with bass.

54. Lobt Gott, ihr Christen, allzugleich

From Cantata 151, "Süsser Trost, mein Jesus kommt", where it closes the composition with the eighth stanza of the hymn.

Heut' schleusst er wieder auf die Thür
zum schönen Paradeis,
der Cherub steht nicht mehr dafür,
Gott sei Lob, Ehr' und Preis,
Gott sei Lob, Ehr' und Preis.

Terry, no. 238, uses his own translation; Schirmer B-R, I, p. 86, presents a translation by the Rev. Emanuel Cronenwett.

Flauto traverso, Oboe d'amore, and *Violino I* play with the soprano; *Violino II,* with the alto; *Viola,* with the tenor; and *Continuo,* with the bass.

55. Wir Christenleut'

This is the closing number of Cantata 110, "Unser Mund sei voll Lachens", where it appears with the fifth stanza as the text:

Alleluja! Alleluja! gelobt sei Gott!
singen wir All' aus unsers Herzens Grunde;
denn Gott hat heut'
gemacht solch' Freud',
der wir vergessen soll'n zu keiner Stunde.

Terry, no. 397, supplies his own English translation.

Tromba I, Flauti traversi I & II, Oboe I, and *Violino I* play with the soprano; *Oboe II* and *Violino II,* with the alto; *Oboe da caccia* and *Viola,* with the tenor; and *Organo* and *Continuo,* with the bass.

56. Christum wir sollen loben schon

This chorale brings to a close Cantata 121, "Christum wir sollen loben schon", with the eighth stanza of the hymn.

> *Lob, Ehr' und Dank sei dir gesagt,*
> *Christ gebor'n von der reinen Magd,*
> *sammt Vater und dem heil'gen Geist*
> *von nun an bis in Ewigkeit.*

Schirmer B-R, I, p. 110f, uses a translation by Richard Massie; Terry, no. 47, uses one by George Macdonald.

The instrumentation is as follows: *Cornetto, Oboe d'amore,* and *Violino I* with soprano; *Trombone I* and *Violino II* with alto; *Trombone II* and *Viola* with tenor; and *Trombone III* and *Continuo* with bass.

57. O Traurigkeit (n.s.)

58. Herzlich lieb hab' ich dich, o Herr

This chorale is found in Cantata 174, "Ich liebe den Höchsten von ganzem Gemüthe", where it brings the work to a close with the first stanza of the hymn.

> *Herzlich lieb hab' ich dich, o Herr,*
> *ich bitt' : woll'st sein von mir nicht fern*
> *mit deiner Hilf' und Gnaden.*
> *Die ganze Welt erfreut mich nicht,*
> *nach Himm'l und Erde frag' ich nicht,*
> *wenn ich dich nur kann haben.*
> *Herr, wenn mir gleich mein Herz zerbricht,*
> *so bist du doch mein' Zuversicht,*
> *mein Heil und meines Herzens Trost,*
> *der mich durch sein Blut hat erlöst.*
> *Herr Jesu Christ, mein Gott und Herr,*
>   *mein Gott und Herr,*
> *in Schanden lass mich nimmermehr!*

Schirmer B-R, I, p. 112f, presents an English translation by Dr. Philip Schaff; Terry, no. 156, presents his own translation.

Oboe I and *Violini I & II* play with the soprano; *Oboe II* and *Violino III*, with the alto; *Taille* and *Viole I, II, & III*, with the tenor; and the *Continuo*, with the bass. In several places the *Taille* pursues a line different from that of the tenor.

59. Herzliebster Jesu, was hast du

From the first part of the "St. John Passion", where it appears with the seventh stanza:

> *O grosse Lieb', o Lieb' ohn' alle Maasse,*
> *die dich gebracht auf diese Marter-Strasse!*
> *Ich lebte mit der Welt in Lust und Freuden,*
> *und du musst leiden!*

Terry, no. 169, offers his own English translation. *Flauti traversi I & II, Oboe I,* and *Violino I* play with the soprano; *Oboe II* and *Violino II,* with the alto; *Viola,* with the tenor; and *Organo* and *Continuo,* with the bass.

60. Ich freue mich in dir

From Cantata 133, "Ich freue mich in dir", where it brings the cantata to a close. It appears there with the fourth stanza of the hymn.

> *Wohlan! so will ich mich*
> *an dich, o Jesu, halten,*
> *und sollte gleich die Welt*
> *in tausend Stücke spalten.*
> *O Jesu! dir, nur dir,*
> *dir leb' ich ganz allein;*
> *auf dich, allein auf dich,*
> *o Jesu, schlaf' ich ein!*

Schirmer B-R, I, p. 100, offers a translation by Dr. Charles N. Boyd. Terry, no. 186, also presents his own translation.

The instrumentation is as follows: *Cornetto, Oboe d'amore I,* and *Violino I* with soprano; *Oboe d'amore II* and *Violino II* with alto; *Viola* with tenor; and *Continuo* with bass.

61. Jesu Leiden, Pein und Tod

This appears as the closing number of Cantata 159, "Sehet, wir geh'n hinauf gen Jerusalem", with the thirty-third stanza of the hymn.

> *Jesu, deine Passion*
> *ist mir lauter Freude,*
> *deine Wunden, Kron' und Hohn*
> *meines Herzens Weide;*
> *meine Seel' auf Rosen geht,*
> *wenn ich d'ran gedenke,*
> *in dem Himmel eine Stätt'*
> *mir deswegen schenke!*

Terry, no. 205, presents his own English translation.

Oboe and *Violino I* play with the soprano; *Violino II*, with the alto; *Viola*, with the tenor; and *Continuo*, with the bass.

62. Wer nur den lieben Gott lässt walten

This chorale is taken from the Wedding Cantata, "Gott ist uns're Zuversicht", where it closes the composition with the words of the following stanza of the hymn:

> *So wandelt froh auf Gottes Wegen,*
> *und was ihr thut, das thut getreu!*
> *Verdienet eures Gottes Segen,*
> *denn der ist alle Morgen neu:*
> *denn welcher seine Zuversicht*
> *auf Gott setzt, den verlässt er nicht.*

Terry, no. 380, indicates for this setting a text beginning "*Sing, bet, und geh auf Gottes Wegen*", which has only the rhymes and the last two lines in common with the text that Bach used; but in his *Joh. Seb. Bach Cantata Texts* (Constable, London) p. 544, he offers his own translation of the correct stanza.

No indication is given in the chorale for the use of the instruments.   Those used for the cantata were no doubt applied in this chorale.   They were as follows: *Trombe I, II, & III, Timpani, Oboi I & II, Oboi d'amore I & II, Fagotto,* Strings, and *Continuo.*

63. Nun ruhen alle Wälder

This is better known under the name "O Welt, ich muss dich lassen".   The harmonization given here is taken from Part I of the "St. John Passion", where it appears with the text of stanzas III and IV.   The use of two stanzas with one harmonization is quite unusual for Bach.

> *Wer hat dich so geschlagen,*
> *mein Heil, und dich mit Plagen*
> *so übel zugericht't?*
> *Du bist ja nicht ein Sünder,*
> *wie wir und unsre Kinder,*
> *von Missethaten weisst du nicht.*
>
> *Ich, ich und meine Sünden,*
> *die sich wie Körnlein finden*
> *des Sandes an dem Meer,*
> *die haben dir erreget*
> *das Elend, das dich schläget,*
> *und das betrübte Marterheer.*

Terry, no. 302, presents his own translations for both stanzas.   Schirmer B-R, I, p. 104, offers a translation by John S. Dwight for stanza III as used with the same tune in the "St. Matthew Passion".

Flauti traversi I & II, Oboi I & II, and *Violino I* play with the soprano; *Violino II*, with the alto; *Viola*, with the tenor; and *Organo* and *Continuo*, with the bass.

64. Freu' dich sehr, o meine Seele

This chorale appears here in the key of G major and, as No. 256 under the name "Jesu, deine tiefen Wunden", in the key of Bb.   In the latter key it forms the closing number of the cantata "Höchsterwünschtes Freudenfest".   Aside from a very slight difference in the second measure and the next-to-last note of the chorale, the harmonizations are identical.   It is safe to assume that the present number has undergone a transposition by the copyist.

In the cantata, *Oboe I, Oboe II, Oboe III, Violino I, Violino II, Viola,* and *Continuo* are given separate staves in the full score.   *Oboe I* and *Violino I* are identical with the soprano; *Oboe II* and *Violino II*, with the alto; *Viola,* with the tenor; and the *Continuo* (except for the usual variations), with the bass.   Only *Oboe III* has an independent part.   The chorale is exceptional in using two stanzas of the hymn (the sixth and seventh):

> VI. *Heil'ger Geist in's Himmels Throne,*
> *gleicher Gott von Ewigkeit*
> *mit dem Vater und dem Sohne,*
> *der Betrübten Trost und Freud'!*
> *Allen Glauben, den ich find',*
> *hast du in mir angezünd't,*
> *über mir in Gnaden walte,*
> *ferner deine Gnad' erhalte.*
>
> VII. *Deine Hülfe zu mir sende,*
> *O du edler Herzensgast!*
> *und das gute Werk vollende,*
> *das du angefangen hast.*
> *Blas' in mir das Fünklein auf,*
> *bis dass nach vollbrachtem Lauf*
> *ich den Auserwählten gleiche*
> *und des Glaubens Ziel erreiche.*

Terry, no. 106, offers his own English translations for both stanzas.

Other harmonizations of the same melody are found in the present collection as Nos. 29, 67, 76, and 282, as well as the one mentioned above as No. 256.

65. Was Gott tut, das ist wohlgetan

From Cantata 144, "Nimm, was dein ist, und gehe hin". Its place is in the middle part of the cantata and it employs as the text the first stanza of the hymn:

Was Gott thut, das ist wohlgethan,
es bleibt gerecht sein Wille;
wie er fängt meine Sachen an,
will ich ihm halten stille.
Er ist mein Gott,
der in der Noth
mich wohl weiss zu erhalten:
drum lass' ich ihn nur walten.

No instruments are indicated. The instruments for the cantata, which are also very sparingly indicated, are *Oboe d'amore*, Strings, and *Continuo*.

Schirmer B-R, I, p. 90, presents an English translation by the Rev. Emanuel Cronenwett. Terry, no. 352, uses his own translation.

66. Christ, unser Herr, zum Jordan kam (n.s.)

Another harmonization is found as No. 119.

67. Freu' dich sehr, o meine Seele

Taken from Cantata 39, "Brich dem Hungrigen dein Brod", where it forms the conclusion of Part II. It uses the sixth stanza of the hymn.

Selig sind, die aus Erbarmen
sich annehmen fremder Noth,
sind mitleidig mit den Armen,
bitten treulich für sie Gott.
Die behülflich sind mit Rath,
auch, wo möglich, mit der That,
werden wieder Hülf' empfangen
und Barmherzigkeit erlangen.

Terry, no. 105, supplies his own translation.

The instrumentation is as follows: *Flauti I & II* in octaves, *Oboi I & II*, and *Violino I* with soprano; *Violino II* with alto; *Viola* with tenor; and *Continuo* with bass.

This is one of the chorales that have been subjected to transposition without any apparent reason. Here it is in G major. In the cantata it appears in B♭.

68. Wenn wir in höchsten Nöten sein (n.s.)

Erk, no. 306, publishes this chorale in G major and he makes strong claims that the copyist of the manuscript upon which the "371" is based took great liberties in transposing many of the numbers from their original key. Smend, no. 278 in his revision of Erk's work, returns to the key of F major.

69. Komm, heiliger Geist, Herre Gott

This is another one of the chorales that were changed by transposition. It is the closing number in the motet for double chorus, "Der Geist hilft unsrer Schwachheit auf". Among the "371" it is in G major, in the motet in B♭.

Du heilige Brunst, süsser Trost,
nun hilf uns fröhlich und getrost
in deinem Dienst beständig bleiben,
die Trübsal uns nicht abtreiben.
O Herr, durch dein' Kraft uns bereit'
und stärk' des Fleisches Blödigkeit,
dass wir hier ritterlich ringen,
durch Tod und Leben zu dir dringen.
Halleluja! Halleluja!

Terry, no. 227, uses the English translation by Catherine Winkworth.

Although it was not customary to use complete instrumental accompaniment with the motets, a set of string parts duplicating the voices of Chorus I and a set of woodwind parts duplicating those of Chorus II are extant, mostly written in Bach's own hand. Also an *Organo* part with exact "figures" in A♭, which is a half-tone lower and takes into account the tuning of the ogans of that day.

70. Gott sei gelobet und gebenedeiet (n. s.)

The low notes in measures 3, 6, and 8 are no doubt due to the influence of the instrumental bass. Erk, no. 213, changes the key to A major. Smend in his revision of Erk's edition returns to G major.

71. Ich ruf' zu dir, Herr Jesu Christ

This brings to a close Cantata 177, "Ich ruf' zu dir, Herr Jesu Christ", where it appears in the key of G minor. For some unknown reason the copyist in preparing the manuscript, which was used as the basis for the "371", selected the key of E minor, a third lower than the original. The vocal bass of the last note should be indicated one octave higher. The text is that of the fifth stanza.

> Ich lieg' im Streit und widerstreb',
> hilf, o Herr Christ, dem Schwachen!
> An deiner Gnad' allein ich kleb',
> du kannst mich stärker machen.
> Kömmt nun Anfechtung, Herr, so wehr',
> dass sie mich nicht umstosse.
> Du kannst maassen,
> dass mir's nicht bring' Gefahr;
> ich weiss, du wirst's nicht lassen.

Oboi I & II and Violino I play with the soprano; Violino II, with the alto; Viola, with the tenor; and Continuo and Fagotto, with the bass.

72. Erhalt' uns, Herr, bei deinem Wort

This is the closing number of Cantata 6, "Bleib' bei uns, denn es will Abend werden". The stanza used is the second:

> Beweis' dein' Macht, Herr Jesu Christ,
> der du Herr aller Herren bist:
> beschirm' dein' arme Christenheit,
> dass sie dich lob' in Ewigkeit.

Schirmer B-R, I, p. 95, uses a translation from the Moravian Hymn Book; Terry, no. 82, presents his own translation.

Violino I and Oboi I & II play with the soprano; Violino II and Oboe di caccia, with the alto; Viola, with the tenor; and Continuo, with the bass.

73. Herr Jesu Christ, du höchstes Gut (n.s.)

Other harmonizations may be found in the present edition as Nos. 266 and 294.

74. O Haupt voll Blut und Wunden

The more prevalent name under which this chorale is known is "Herzlich thut mich ver-langen". It is found in the "St. Matthew Passion", where the melody is harmonized five times. The text is the first stanza of "O Haupt voll Blut und Wunden"; hence the title by which it appears in the "371", in preference to its original name. Other names under which this tune was known are "Ach Herr, mich armen Sünder", "Befiehl du deine Wege", and "Wie soll ich dich empfangen". The second stanza of the hymn was also used for this setting.

I. O Haupt voll Blut und Wunden,
   voll Schmerz und voller Hohn!
   O Haupt, zu Spott gebunden
   mit einer Dornenkron'!
   O Haupt, sonst schön gezieret
   mit höchster Ehr' und Zier,
   jetzt aber hoch schimpfiret:
   gegrüsset seist du mir!

II. Du edles Angesichte,
    vor dem sonst schrickt und scheut
    das grosse Weltgerichte,
    wie bist du so bespeit!
    Wie bist du so erbleichet,
    wer hat dein Augenlicht,
    dem sonst kein Licht nicht gleichet,
    so schändlich zugericht't?

Schirmer B-R, I, p. 84, uses an English translation by John S. Dwight; Terry, no. 168, uses one by J. W. Alexander.

Flauti traversi I & II, Oboi I & II, and Violino I play with the soprano; Violino II, with the alto; Viola, with the tenor; and Organo and Continuo, with the bass.

75. Das walt' mein Gott (n. s.)

This tune was comparatively rare in its use. The low bass notes in the fourth and fifth measures are no doubt derived from the instrumental bass.

76. Freu' dich sehr, o meine Seele

This chorale brings to a close the first part of Cantata 30, "Freue dich, erlöste Schaar". In the cantata the key is A major; in the "371" it is G major. The text is the third stanza:

> Eine Stimme lässt sich hören
> in der Wüsten, weit und breit,

alle Menschen zu bekehren:
macht dem Herrn den Weg bereit,
machet Gott ein' eb'ne Bahn,
alle Welt soll heben an,
alle Thäler zu erhöhen,
dass die Berge niedrig stehen.

Schirmer B-R, I, p. 111, offers the English translation by Catherine Winkworth.

Flauti traversi I & II in octaves, *Oboi I & II,* and *Violino I* play with the soprano; *Violino II,* with the alto; *Viola,* with the tenor; and *Organo* and *Continuo,* with the bass.

77. In dich hab' ich gehoffet, Herr

This chorale is from the "Christmas Oratorio", where it occupies a middle position in Part V. The stanza is the sixth:

> *Dein Glanz all' Finsterniss verzehrt,*
> *die trübe Nacht in Licht verkehrt.*
> *Leit' uns auf deinen Wegen,*
> *dass dein Gesicht*
> *und herrlich's Licht*
> *wir ewig schauen mögen!*

Terry, no. 194, offers his own translation.

Oboi d'amore I & II and *Violino I* play with the soprano; *Violino II,* with the alto; *Viola,* with the tenor; and *Organo* and *Continuo,* with the bass.

78. Herzliebster Jesu, was hast du

This chorale makes its appearance early in the "St. Matthew Passion".

The stanza is the first one:

> *Herzliebster Jesu, was hast du verbrochen,*
> *dass man ein solch hart Urtheil hat gesprochen?*
> *Was ist die Schuld, in was für Missethaten bist du gerathen?*

In most translations, a bit of tone-painting in the eighth and ninth measures where Bach describes the word *Missethaten* ("transgressions") by a descending figure covering the interval of a diminished eleventh is entirely lost by a wrong placing of the words. Schirmer B-R, I, p. 85, uses a revised version of the translation by Catherine Winkworth.

Violino I, Flauti traversi, and *Oboi* play with the soprano; *Violino II,* with the alto; *Viola,* with the tenor; and *Organo* and *Continuo,* with the bass.

79. Heut' triumphieret Gottes Sohn (n.s.)

Another harmonization of this chorale in the more elaborate idiom of the organ may be found as no. 32 of the *Orgelbüchlein.*

80. O Haupt voll Blut und Wunden

This is the one of five harmonizations of "Herzlich thut mich verlangen" to be found in the "St. Matthew Passion". The words used are the first stanza of the hymn "Befiehl du deine Wege":

> *Befiehl du deine Wege*
> *und was dein Herze kränkt*
> *der allertreusten Pflege*
> *dess, der den Himmel lenkt;*
> *der Wolken, Luft und Winden*
> *giebt Wege, Lauf und Bahn,*
> *der wird auch Wege finden,*
> *da dein Fuss gehen kann.*

Schirmer B-R, I, p. 84, uses the John S. Dwight translation. Terry, no. 165, offers his own translation.

Flauti traversi I & II, Oboi I & II, and *Violino I* play with the soprano; *Violino II,* with the alto; *Viola,* with the tenor; and *Organo* and *Continuo,* with the bass.

81. Christus, der uns selig macht

This chorale opens the second part of the "St. John Passion". The text is the first stanza of the hymn.

> *Christus, der uns selig macht,*
> *kein Bös's hat begangen,*
> *der ward für uns in der Nacht*
> *als ein Dieb gefangen,*
> *geführt vor gottlose Leut'*
> *und fälschlich verklaget,*
> *verlacht, verhöhnt und verspeit,*
> *wie denn die Schrift saget.*

Schirmer B-R, I. p. 80, uses an English translation by the author of these notes. Terry, no. 51, presents his own translation.

Flauti traversi I & II, *Oboe I*, and *Violino I* play with the soprano; *Oboe II* and *Violino II*, with the alto; *Viola*, with the tenor; and *Organo* and *Continuo*, with the bass.

82. O grosser Gott von Macht

This chorale, with a fairly elaborate obbligato of orchestral instruments and interludes, brings to conclusion Cantata 46, "Schauet doch und sehet, ob irgend ein Schmerz sei". The text is the ninth stanza:

> *O grosser Gott der Treu ,*
> *weil vor dir Niemand gilt*
> *als dein Sohn Jesus Christ,*
> *der deinen Zorn gestillt:*
> *so sieh' doch an die Wunden sein,*
> *sein' Marter, Angst und schwere Pein.*
> *Um seinetwillen schone,*
> *und nicht nach Sünden lohne.*

Schirmer B-R, II, no. 112, presents a splendid English translation by Charles N. Boyd. Terry, no. 291, presents his own translation of this stanza, as well as of three additional ones.

The elimination of the interludes has caused some destruction of the rhythmic values. The second verse-line, as well as the fifth, begin on the fourth beat in this version, whereas in the original they begin on the second beat. The sixth verse-line begins in this version on the second beat, in the original on the fourth beat.

The original version has the *Tromba* or *Corno da tirarsi* playing with the soprano while the *Continuo* elaborates the bass. *Violino I*, *Violino II*, and *Viola* parts duplicate the soprano, alto, and tenor parts, respectively, on separate staves of the score, but enliven the movement by playing in eighth notes. The most elaborate parts·are assigned to the first and second flutes, which have florid independent parts continuing between the verse-lines of the chorale to form the interludes. These were probably *flûtes à bec*, and Bach's added notation "*a due*" would indicate the necessity for strengthening the flute parts. Autograph copies of *Oboi* parts to duplicate the flutes are also in existence. The chorale, as laid out in the score, is a splendid example of six-part writing.

83. Jesu Leiden, Pein und Tod

This chorale brings to a close the first part of the "St. John Passion" with the words of the tenth stanza:

> *Petrus, der nicht denkt zurück,*
> *seinen Gott verneinet,*
> *der doch auf ein'n ernsten Blick*
> *bitterlichen weinet:*
> *Jesu, blicke mich auch an,*
> *wenn ich nicht will büssen;*
> *wenn ich Böses hab' gethan,*
> *rühre mein Gewissen.*

Terry, no. 206, uses his own translation; and Schirmer B-R, I, 85, presents a translation by the author of these notes.

Flauti traversi I & II, *Oboe I*, and *Violino I* play with the soprano; *Oboe II* and *Violino II*, with the alto; *Viola*, with the tenor; and *Organo* and *Continuo*, with the bass. In the fourteenth measure the Viola fills out the chord with an F♯.

84. Nun bitten wir den heiligen Geist

This chorale forms the conclusion of the first part of the Wedding Cantata, "Gott ist uns're Zuversicht". It is the part that was usually performed before the wedding ceremony. It appears with the third stanza of the hymn.

> *Du süsse Lieb', schenk' uns deine Gunst,*
> *lass uns empfinden der Liebe Brunst,*
> *dass wir von Herzen einander lieben,*
> *und in Fried' auf einem Sinne bleiben.*
> *Kyrie eleis!*

Schirmer B-R, I, p. 123, uses an anonymous translation. Terry, no. 264, uses one by George Macdonald.

No indications for the instruments to be used with the chorale are given. Those for the cantata are as follows: *Trombe I, II, & III*, *Timpani*, *Oboi I & II*, *Oboi d'amore I & II*, *Fagotto obbligato*, Strings, and *Continuo*.

85. O Gott, du frommer Gott

This is the closing number of Cantata 45, "Es ist dir gesagt, Mensch, was gut ist". The second stanza of the hymn is used.

Gieb, dass ich thu' mit Fleiss,
was mir zu thun gebühret,
wozu mich dein Befehl
in meinem Stande führet.
Gieb, dass ich's thue bald,
zu der Zeit, da ich soll;
und wenn ich's thu', so gieb,
dass es gerathe wohl.

Schirmer B-R, I, p. 103, uses a translation by Catherine Winkworth. Terry, no. 287, employs his own translation.

Flauti traversi I & II, Oboi I & II, and *Violino I* parallel the soprano; *Violino II,* the alto; *Viola,* the tenor; and *Continuo,* the bass.

Sometimes this tune is called "Was frag' ich nach der Welt". Two harmonizations under this name are found in this set: Nos. 255 and 291.

86. Wie schön leuchtet der Morgenstern

This chorale closes the first part of Cantata 36, "Schwingt freudig euch empor", where it appears with the sixth stanza:

Zwingt die Saiten in Cythara
und lasst die süsse Musica
ganz freudenreich erschallen,
dass ich möge mit Jesulein,
dem wunderschönen Bräut'gam mein,
in steter Liebe wallen.
Singet,
springet,
jubiliret,
triumphiret,
dankt dem Herren!
Gross ist der König der Ehren.

Terry, no. 390, offers his own translation.

Oboe d'amore I and *Violino I* play the soprano part; *Oboe d'amore II* and *Violino II,* the alto; *Viola,* the tenor; and *Organo* and *Continuo,* the bass.

This edition offers a unique opportunity for comparison. The present number, No. 195, and No. 305 are identical harmonizations. This was not always so. In the 1786 and 1787 edition the last alto and soprano notes of the eighth measure and almost all of the ninth measure were different in these latter two mentioned chorales. They were wrongly changed in the 1831 edition so that since that time three identical chorale harmoniza-

tions, based upon the same melody, have appeared among the "371".

87. Du, o schönes Weltgebäude

This chorale forms the closing number of the bass solo Cantata 56, "Ich will den Kreuzstab", where it appears with the sixth stanza:

Komm, o Tod, du Schlafes Bruder,
komm, und führe mich nur fort;
löse meines Schiffleins Ruder,
bringe mich an sichern Port.
Es mag, wer da will, dich scheuen,
du kannst mich vielmehr erfreuen;
denn durch dich komm' ich hinein
zu dem schönsten Jesulein.

An English translation by Dr. Charles N. Boyd is used in Schirmer B-R, I, p. 81. Terry, no. 74, presents his own translation.

Oboi I & II and *Violino I* play with the soprano; *Violino II,* with the alto; *Taille* and *Viola,* with the tenor; and *Continuo,* with the bass.

88. Helft mir Gott's Güte preisen

This harmonization is identical with that of No. 23, where the chorale was incorrectly named as "Zeuch ein zu deinen Toren".

89. O Haupt voll Blut und Wunden

This chorale, which is usually known under the name "Herzlich thut mich verlangen", appears towards the end of the "St. Matthew Passion" with the text of the ninth stanza of the hymn "O Haupt voll Blut und Wunden".

Wenn ich einmal soll scheiden,
so scheide nicht von mir!
Wenn ich den Tod soll leiden,
so tritt du dann herfür!
Wenn mir am allerbängsten
wird um das Herze sein,
so reiss mich aus den Aengsten
kraft deiner Angst und Pein!

Schirmer B-R, I, p. 84, uses the English translation by John S. Dwight. Terry, no. 160, presents his own translation.

Flauti traversi I & II, Oboi I & II, and *Violino I* play with the soprano; *Violino II,* with the alto; *Viola*, with the tenor; and *Organo* and *Continuo*, with the bass.

This chorale appears here with a two-sharp signature. In its source, the "St. Matthew Passion", it appears with no sharps or flats, thus giving it certain aspects of beginning in the Aeolian mode and passing into the Phrygian.

90. Hast du denn, Jesu, dein Angesicht

This chorale is more commonly known under the name "Lobe den Herren, den mächtigen König der Ehren". This melody has been treated quite freely by Bach, no 18th-century melodic text of this chorale being known that is identical with the one here. It forms the closing number of Cantata 57, "Selig ist der Mann", and appears with the sixth stanza:

> *Richte dich, Liebste, nach meinem Gefallen*
> *und gläube,*
> *dass ich dein Seelenfreund immer und ewig*
> *verbleibe,*
> *der dich ergötzt,*
> *und in den Himmel versetzt*
> *aus dem gemarterten Leibe.*

Terry, no. 125, presents his own translation.
Oboe I and *Violino I* play with the soprano; *Oboe II* and *Violino II*, with the alto; *Taille* and *Viola*, with the tenor; and *Organo* and *Continuo*, with the bass.

91. Verleih' uns Frieden gnädiglich

This chorale brings to a close Cantata 42, "Am Abend aber desselbigen Sabbaths", where it appears with the following stanza:

> *Verleih' uns Frieden gnädiglich,*
> *Herr Gott, zu unsern Zeiten,*
> *es ist ja doch kein Andrer nicht,*
> *der für uns könnte streiten,*
> *denn du, uns'r Gott alleine.*
> *Gieb unsern Fürsten und der Obrigkeit*
> *Fried' und gut Regiment,*
> *dass wir unter ihnen*
> *ein geruhig und stilles Leben führen mögen*
> *in aller Gottseligkeit*
> *und Ehrbarkeit, Amen!*

Terry, no. 332, uses his own translation. Schirmer B-R, I, p. 125, uses a translation by the author of these notes.

Oboi I & II and *Violino I* play with the soprano; *Violino II*, with the alto; *Viola*, with the tenor; and *Fagotto*, *Organo*, and *Continuo*, with the bass.

92. O Jesu Christ, du höchstes Gut

This chorale is known under the name "Herr Jesu Christ, du höchstes Gut", where it brings to a close the solo Cantata 168, "Thue Rechnung! Donnerwort". The text is the eighth stanza:

> *Stärk' mich mit deinem Freudengeist,*
> *heil' mich mit deinen Wunden,*
> *wasch' mich mit deinem Todesschweiss*
> *in meinen letzten Stunden;*
> *und nimm mich einst, wenn dir's gefällt,*
> *in wahrem Glauben von der Welt*
> *zu deinen Auserwählten.*

Terry, no. 147, uses his own English translation.
Oboi d'amore I & II and *Violino I* play with the soprano; *Violino II*, with the alto; *Viola*, with the tenor; and the *Continuo*, with the bass.

93. Wach' auf, mein Herz

This chorale is more commonly known as "Nun lasst uns Gott, dem Herren". In No. 257 will be found this identical harmonization under that name. This chorale closes the cantata "Höchsterwunschtes Freudenfest". Bach uses the text of two stanzas, the ninth and the tenth:

> IX. *Sprich Ja zu meinen Thaten,*
> *hilf selbst das Beste rathen;*
> *den Anfang, Mitt'l und Ende,*
> *ach Herr, zum Besten wende.*

> X. *Mit Segen mich beschütte,*
> *mein Herz sei deine Hütte,*
> *dein Wort sei meine Speise,*
> *bis ich gen Himmel reise.*

Terry, no. 275, presents his own translation.
The instruments, *Oboe I*, *Oboe II*, *Oboe III*, *Violino I*, *Violino II*, and *Viola*, are written upon separate staves. Only the *Oboe III* is an independent part. *Oboe I* and *Violino I* play with the soprano; *Oboe II* and *Violino II*, with the alto; *Viola*, with the tenor; and *Continuo*, with the bass.

94. Warum betrübst du dich, mein Herz

This closes Cantata 47, "Wer sich selbst erhöhet, der soll erniedriget werden", with the eleventh stanza:

Der zeitlichen Ehr' will ich gern entbehr'n,
du woll'st mir nur das Ew'ge gewähr'n,
das du erworben hast
durch deinen herben, bittern Tod.
Das bitt' ich dich, mein Herr und Gott!

Schirmer B-R, I, p. 108, uses a translation by Catherine Winkworth. Terry, no. 344, furnishes his own translation.

Oboi I & II and *Violino I* play with the soprano; *Violino II*, with the alto; *Viola*, with the tenor; and *Continuo*, with the bass.

95. Werde munter, mein Gemüte

This is the closing number of the tenor solo Cantata 55, "Ich armer Mensch, ich Sündenknecht". The text is the sixth stanza:

Bin ich gleich von dir gewichen,
stell' ich mich doch wieder ein;
hat uns doch dein Sohn verglichen
durch sein' Angst und Todespein.
Ich verleugne nicht die Schuld,
aber deine Gnad' und Huld
ist viel grösser als die Sünde,
die ich stets in mir befinde.

Schirmer B-R, I, p. 127, uses an English translation of this stanza by Dr. Emanuel Cronenwett, for a different harmonization. Terry, no. 387, presents a translation by Catherine Winkworth.

Flauto traverso, Oboe, and *Violino I* combine with the soprano; *Violino II,* with the alto; *Viola,* with the tenor; and *Continuo,* with the bass.

96. Jesu, meine Freude

This is the closing number of Cantata 87 for alto, tenor, and bass soli, "Bisher habt ihr nichts gebeten in meinem Namen". It appears with the ninth stanza:

Muss ich sein betrübet?
so mich Jesus liebet,
ist mir aller Schmerz
über Honig süsse,

tausend Zuckerküsse
drücket er an's Herz.
Wenn die Pein
sich stellet ein,
seine Liebe macht zur Freuden
auch das bitt're Leiden.

Terry, no. 209, offers an original translation of the stanza.

Oboe I and *Violino I* play with the soprano; *Oboe da caccia I* and *Violino II*, with the alto; *Oboe da caccia II* and *Viola*, with the tenor; and *Continuo*, with the bass.

Bach wrote this in a signature without flats or sharps, giving it a Dorian basis. In the "371" one flat has been added to the signature.

97. Nun bitten wir den heiligen Geist

This composition closes Cantata 169, "Gott soll allein mein Herze haben", with the third stanza of the hymn.

Du süsse Liebe, schenk' uns deine Gunst,
lass uns empfinden der Liebe Brunst,
dass wir uns von Herzen einander lieben
und in Frieden auf einem Sinn bleiben.
Kyrie eleison.

Schirmer B-R, I, p. 123, presents an English translation by an anonymous writer Terry, no. 262, presents one by George Macdonald.

Oboi I & II and *Violino I* play with the soprano; *Violino II*, with the alto; *Taille* and *Viola* with the tenor; and *Continuo*, with the bass.

98. O Haupt voll Blut und Wunden

This is from the "St. Matthew Passion", where it appears first in the key of E major to the words "Erkenne mich, mein Hüter". After a short recitative, the subject of which deals with the denial of Jesus by his disciples, it appears a halftone lower, in E♭ major, to the words "Ich will hier bei dir stehen". The natural reaction of the denouement is one of depression, and Bach makes use of a slight lowering of the pitch of the chorale to depict this feeling. It is curious to find that for the "371" the copyist selected neither of these keys, but transposed the chorale to the key of D major.

V. *Erkenne mich, mein Hüter,*
    mein Hirte, nimm mich an,

von dir, Quell aller Güter,
ist mir viel Gut's gethan.
Dein Mund hat mich gelabet
mit Milch und süsser Kost,
dein Geist hat mich begabet
mit mancher Himmelslust.

VI.   *Ich will hier bei dir stehen:*
verachte mich doch nicht!
Von dir will ich nicht gehen,
wenn dir dein Herze bricht.
Wann dein Herz wird erblassen
im letzten Todesstoss,
alsdann will ich dich fassen
in meinen Arm und Schooss.

In the E major version, *Flauti traversi I & II,*
Oboi I & II, and *Violino I* play with the soprano;
Violino II, with the alto; *Viola*, with the tenor;
and *Organo* and *Continuo*, with the bass. In the
second version, in E♭ major, Bach omits the
flutes in order to enhance the sombre and de-
pressed feeling caused by lowering the pitch in
its repetition.

Schirmer B-R, I, p. 83, presents an English
translation of the first stanza by John S. Dwight
and of the second stanza by Dr. James W. Alexander. Terry, no. 167, presents his own translation of both stanzas.

99. Helft mir Gott's Güte preisen

This chorale brings to a close Cantata 16,
"Herr Gott dich loben wir". The stanza of the
hymn is the sixth:

All solch dein Güt' wir preisen,
Vater in's Himmels Thron,
die du uns thust beweisen
durch Jesum deinen Sohn,
und bitten ferner dich,
gieb uns ein friedlich Jahre,
vor alles Leid bewahre
und nähr' uns mildiglich.

Schirmer B-R, I, p. 97, uses the translation by
J. C. Jacobi.
Corno di caccia, Oboe I, and *Violino I* play with
the soprano; *Oboe II* and *Violino II*, with the
alto; no indication is given for the tenor, but it is
no doubt the *Viola; Continuo* plays with the bass.

100. Durch Adams Fall ist ganz verderbt

This chorale closes Cantata 18, "Gleich wie
der Regen und Schnee vom Himmel fällt". The
stanza is the eighth. An identical harmonization is found in this edition as No. 126 but transposed to the key of A minor.

Ich bitt' o Herr, aus Herzens Grund,
du wollst nicht von mir nehmen
dein heil'ges Wort aus meinem Mund;
so wird mich nicht beschämen
mein' Sünd' und Schuld,
denn in dein' Huld
setz' ich all mein Vertrauen.
Wer sich nur fest
darauf verlässt,
der wird den Tod nicht schauen.

Schirmer B-R, I, p. 94, uses a translation by J.
C. Jacobi. Terry, no. 76, presents his own
translation.
Flauti I & II and *Viole I & II* play with the
soprano; *Viola III*, with the alto; *Viola IV*, with
the tenor; and *Fagotto* and *Continuo*, with the
bass. It is of interest to note that no Violins
are scored for this cantata.

101. Herr Christ, der ein'ge Gott's-Sohn

This chorale forms the closing number of Cantata 164, "Ihr, die ihr euch von Christo nennet",
with the fifth stanza:

Ertödt' uns durch dein' Güte,
erweck' uns durch dein' Gnad'!
Den alten Menschen kränke,
dass der neu leben mag
wohl hier auf dieser Erden,
der Sinn und all Begehrden,
nur G'danken hab' zu dir.

In Schirmer B-R, I, p. 82, where the same stanza
is used for another harmonization, may be found
an English translation by Bishop Miles Coverdale (1539). Terry, no. 132, uses his own translation.
Oboi I & II and *Violino I* take the soprano
part; *Violino II*, the alto; *Viola*, the tenor; and
Continuo, the bass.

102. Ermuntre dich, mein schwacher Geist

This is taken from Cantata 43, "Gott fähret
auf mit Jauchzen", where it appears as the closing number with the first and thirteenth stanzas:

I. *Du Lebensfürst, Herr Jesu Christ,*
der du bist aufgenommen
gen Himmel, da dein Vater ist
und die Gemein' der Frommen:
wie soll ich deinen grossen Sieg,
den du durch einen schweren Krieg
erworben hast, recht preisen,
und dir g'nug Ehr' erweisen?

XIII. *Zieh' uns dir nach, so laufen wir,*
gieb uns des Glaubens Flügel!
Hilf, dass wir fliehen weit von hier
auf Israelis Hügel.
Mein Gott! wann fahr' ich doch dahin,
woselbst ich ewig fröhlich bin?
wann werd' ich vor dir stehen,
dein Angesicht zu sehen?

Terry, no. 85, uses his own English translation.
Trombe I & II, Oboi I & II, and *Violino I* agree with the soprano; *Tromba III* and *Violino II,* with the alto; *Viola,* with the tenor; and *Continuo,* with the bass. In the twelfth measure and in the preceding one, Terry presents a different version of the alto.

103. Nun ruhen alle Wälder

The more common name for this chorale is "O Welt, ich muss dich lassen". It is taken from Cantata 13, "Meine Seufzer, meine Thränen", where it appears with the text of the fifteenth stanza as the closing number of the cantata.

So sei nun Seele deine,
und traue dem alleine,
der dich erschaffen hat.
Es gehe wie es gehe,
dein Vater in der Höhe,
der weiss zu allen Sachen Rath.

Terry, no. 307, offers his own translation.
Flauti, Oboe, and *Violino I* play with the soprano; *Violino II,* with the alto; *Viola,* with the tenor; and *Continuo,* with the bass.

104. Wer nur den lieben Gott lässt walten

This chorale, with the text of the eighth stanza, ends Cantata 88, "Siehe, ich will viel Fischer aussenden, spricht der Herr".

Sing', bet' und geh' auf Gottes Wegen,
verricht' das Deine nur getreu,

und trau' des Himmels reichem Segen,
so wird er bei dir werden neu:
denn welcher seine Zuversicht
auf Gott setzt, den verlässt er nicht.

Schirmer B-R, I, p. 91, presents an English translation by Catherine Winkworth; Terry, no. 379, presents his own translation.
Oboi d'amore I & II and *Violino I* play with the soprano; *Taille* and *Violino II,* with the alto; *Viola,* with the tenor; and *Continuo,* with the bass.

105. Herzliebster Jesu, was hast du verbrochen

This chorale appears with the text of the fourth stanza in the latter half of the "St. Matthew Passion":

Wie wunderbarlich ist doch diese Strafe!
der gute Hirte leidet für die Schaafe;
die Schuld bezahlt der Herre, der Gerechte,
für seine Knechte!

Terry, no. 172, offers the English translation by Catherine Winkworth.
Flauti traversi I & II, Oboi I & II, and *Violino I* play with the soprano; *Violino II,* with the alto; *Viola,* with the tenor; and *Organo* and *Continuo,* with the bass.

106. Jesu Leiden, Pein und Tod

This is one of the last chorales in the "St. John Passion", where it is associated with the twentieth stanza of the hymn.

Er nahm Alles wohl in Acht
in der letzten Stunde,
seine Mutter noch bedacht',
setzt ihr ein'n Vormunde.
O Mensch, mache Richtigkeit,
Gott und Menschen liebe,
stirb darauf ohn' alles Leid,
und dich nicht betrübe!

Terry, no. 207, presents an original translation.
Flauti traversi I & II, Oboi I & II, and *Violino I* follow the soprano part; *Violino II,* the alto; *Viola,* the tenor; and *Organo* and *Continuo,* the bass.

107.   Herzlich lieb hab' ich dich, o Herr

This wonderful chorale brings to a close the "St. John Passion", with the text of the third stanza. It is one of Bach's most noteworthy examples of truly inspired chorale harmonization, if one may be so bold as to make such a selection among such a great treasure store.

> *Ach Herr, lass dein lieb' Engelein*
> *am letzten End' die Seele mein*
> *in Abrahams Schooss tragen;*
> *den Leib in sein'm Schlafkämmerlein*
> *gar sanft, ohn ein'ge Qual und Pein,*
> *ruhn bis am jüngsten Tage!*
> *Alsdann vom Tod erwecke mich,*
> *dass meine Augen sehen dich*
> *in aller Freud', o Gottes Sohn,*
> *mein Heiland und Genadenthron!*
> *Herr Jesu Christ, erhöre mich, erhöre mich,*
> *ich will dich preisen ewiglich!*

Terry, no. 157, offers his own English translation.
Flauto traverso I, Oboe I, and *Violino I* play with the soprano; *Flauto traverso II, Oboe II*, and *Violino II*, with the alto; *Viola*, with the tenor; and *Organo* and *Continuo*, with the bass.

108.   Valet will ich dir geben

This chorale is found in Part II of the "St. John Passion", with the third stanza of the hymn.

> *In meines Herzens Grunde,*
> *dein Nam' und Kreuz allein*
> *funkelt allzeit und Stunde,*
> *drauf kann ich fröhlich sein.*
> *Erschein' mir in dem Bilde*
> *zu Trost in meiner Noth,*
> *wie du, Herr Christ, so milde*
> *dich hast geblut't zu Tod.*

Schirmer B-R, I, p. 89, uses an English translation by Catherine Winkworth; Terry, no. 325, presents his own translation.
The instruments were used as follows: *Flauti traversi I & II, Oboi I & II*, and *Violino I* with the soprano; *Violino II* with the alto; *Viola* with the tenor; and *Organo* and *Continuo* with the bass.

109.   Singen wir aus Herzens Grund

In this chorale, which brings to a conclusion Cantata 187, "Es wartet Alles auf dich", we find one of those relatively few instances when Bach uses two stanzas of a hymn.   Here they are the fourth and sixth:

> IV.   *Gott hat die Erd' schön zugericht't,*
> *lässt's an Nahrung mangeln nicht;*
> *Berg und Thal, die macht er nass,*
> *dass dem Vieh auch wächst sein Gras;*
> *aus der Erden Wein und Brod*
> *schaffet Gott, und giebt's uns satt,*
> *dass der Mensch sein Leben hat.*

> VI.   *Wir danken sehr und bitten ihn,*
> *dass er uns geb' des Geistes Sinn,*
> *dass wir solches recht versteh'n,*
> *stets nach sein'n Geboten geh'n,*
> *seinen Namen machen gross*
> *in Christo ohn' Unterlass:*
> *so sing'n wir das Gratias.*

Schirmer B-R, I, p. 124, presents an original translation for both verses by the author of these notes.   Terry, no. 319, uses his own translation.
With the soprano, the following instruments agree: *Oboi I & II* and *Violino I*; with the alto, *Violino II*; with the tenor, *Viola*; and, with the bass, the *Continuo* part.

110.   Vater unser im Himmelreich

Again we have an example of Bach's use of two stanzas of the hymn, namely the sixth and seventh.   The chorale is from Cantata 102, "Herr, deine Augen sehen nach dem Glauben". It is, as usual, the closing number of the cantata.

> VI.   *Heut' lebst du, heut' bekehre dich,*
> *eh' morgen kommt, kann's ändern sich:*
> *wer heut' ist frisch, gesund und roth,*
> *ist morgen krank, ja wohl gar todt.*
> *So du nun stirbest ohne Buss',*
> *dein Leib und Seel' dort brennen muss.*

> VII.   *Hilf, o Herr Jesu, hilf du mir,*
> *dass ich noch heute komm' zu dir*
> *und Busse thu' den Augenblick,*
> *eh' mich der schnelle Tod hinrück':*
> *auf dass ich heut' und jederzeit*
> *zu meiner Heimfahrt sei bereit.*

Terry supplies his own translations in his number 326.

Flauto traverso (in 8va), Oboi I & II, and *Violino I* play with the soprano; *Violino II,* with the alto; *Viola,* with the tenor; and *Continuo,* with the bass.

111. Herzliebster Jesu, was hast du ver- brochen

This chorale, from the "St. John Passion", also uses two stanzas, the eighth and ninth:

VIII. *Ach, grosser König, gross zu allen Zeiten,*
wie kann ich g'nugsam diese Treu' ausbreiten?
Kein's Menschen Herze mag indess ausdenken,
was dir zu schenken.

IX. *Ich kann's mit meinen Sinnen nicht erreichen,*
womit doch dein Erbarmen zu ver- gleichen.
Wie kann ich dir denn deine Liebes- thaten
im ·Werk erstatten?

Terry gives his own translations for both stanzas in his number 170.

Flauti traversi I & II, Oboe I, and *Violino I* play with the soprano; *Oboe II* and *Violino II,* with the alto; *Viola,* with the tenor; and *Organo* and *Continuo,* with the bass.

112. Wer nur den lieben Gott lässt walten

This chorale forms the closing number of Can- tata 84, "Ich bin vergnügt mit meinem Glücke" The twelfth stanza of the hymn is used.

Ich leb' indess in dir vergnüget,
und sterb' ohn' alle Kümmerniss,
mir g'nüget, wie es mein Gott füget,
ich glaub' und bin es ganz gewiss:
durch deine Gnad' und Christi Blut
machst du's mit meinem Ende gut.

Terry offers his own translation in his number 381.

Oboe and *Violino I* play with the soprano; *Violino II,* with the alto; *Viola,* with the tenor; and *Continuo,* with the bass.

113. Christus, der uns selig macht

This chorale, with the eighth stanza of the hymn, appears towards the close of the "St. John Passion".

O hilf, Christe, Gottes Sohn,
durch dein bittres Leiden,
dass wir, dir stets unterthan,
all' Untugend meiden;
deinen Tod und sein' Ursach'
fruchtbarlich bedenken,
dafür, wiewohl arm und schwach,
dir Dankopfer schenken.

Terry presents his own translation in his number 52.

Flauti traversi I & II, Oboi I & II, and *Violino I* play with the soprano; *Violino II,* with the alto; *Viola,* with the tenor; and *Organo* and *Con- tinuo,* with the bass.

114. Von Gott will ich nicht lassen (n.s.)

115. Was mein Gott will, das

This chorale appears with the first stanza of the hymn in Part I of the "St. Matthew Passion"

Was mein Gott will, das g'scheh' allzeit,
sein Will' der ist der beste;
zu helfen den'n er ist bereit,
die an ihn glauben feste;
er hilft aus Noth, der fromme Gott,
und züchtiget mit Maassen.
Wer Gott vertraut,
fest auf ihn baut,
den will er nicht verlassen.

Terry, no. 362, presents his own translation.

Flauti traversi I & II, Oboi I & II, and *Violino I* play with the soprano; *Violino II,* with the alto; *Viola,* with the tenor; and *Organo* and *Continuo,* with the bass.

Neither the photostatic copy of the manu- script nor the Bachgesellschaft Edition have a G♯ before the last tenor note of the seventh measure. Terry adopts the G♮, while Richter maintains the G♯ of the present edition.

116. Nun lob', mein' Seel', den Herren

This chorale, which has been considerably reduced from the original score, brings to a close

Cantata 29, "Wir danken dir, Gott, wir danken dir". It appears there with the fifth stanza:

Sei Lob und Preis mit Ehren,
Gott Vater, Sohn, heiligem Geist!
Der woll' in uns vermehren,
was er uns aus Gnaden verheisst,
dass wir ihm fest vertrauen,
gänzlich verlass'n auf ihn,
von Herzen auf ihn bauen,
dass uns'r Herz, Muth und Sinn
ihm tröstlich soll'n anhangen;
drauf singen wir zur Stund :
Amen! wir werden's erlangen,
glaub'n wir aus Herzens Grund.

Schirmer B-R, book II, no. 111, offers a translation by the author of these notes. Terry, no. 279, uses his own translation.

In the score of the cantata, *Oboi I & II*, on a separate staff, together with *Violino I*, also on a separate staff, duplicate the soprano part; *Violino II*, *Viola*, and *Organo e Continuo* are also placed upon separate staves, duplicating the alto, tenor, and bass respectively. An entirely independent group, consisting of *Trombe I, II, & III* and *Timpani*, are given an important part at the opening of the chorale up to the repeat. This group again enters during the final six measures of the chorale, lending the composition a more festive air than it has in this version.

117. Nun ruhen alle Wälder

This chorale will be recognized under its more prevailing name, "O Welt, ich muss dich lassen". It appears, with the fifth stanza as the text, in the first part of the "St. Matthew Passion".

Ich bin's, ich sollte büssen,
an Händen und an Füssen
gebunden in der Höll'.
Die Geisseln und die Banden,
und was du ausgestanden,
das hat verdienet meine Seel'.

Terry, no. 301, offers his own translation.
Oboi I & II and *Violino I* play with the soprano; *Violino II*, with the alto; *Viola*, with the tenor; and *Organo* and *Continuo*, with the bass.

118. In dich hab' ich gehoffet, Herr

This chorale, with the text of the fifth stanza

of the hymn, is found in Part II of the "St. Matthew Passion".

Mir hat die Welt trüglich gericht't
mit Lügen und mit falschem G'dicht,
viel Netz und heimlich Stricken.
Herr, nimm mein wahr in dieser G'fahr,
b'hüt' mich vor falschen Tücken.

Terry offers his own translation in his number 195.

Flauti traversi I & II, *Oboi I & II*, and *Violino I* play with the soprano; *Violino II*, with the alto; *Viola*, with the tenor; and *Organo* and *Continuo*, with the bass.

119. Christ, unser Herr, zum Jordan kam

This chorale brings to a close Cantata 176, "Es ist ein trotzig und verzagt Ding", with the words of stanza eight as the text:

Auf dass wir also allzugleich
zur Himmelspforte dringen
und dermaleinst in deinem Reich
ohn' alles Ende singen:
dass du alleine König seist,
hoch über alle Götter,
Gott Vater, Sohn und heil'ger Geist,
der Frommen Schutz und Retter—
ein Wesen, drei Personen.

Oboe I and *Violino I* play with the soprano; *Oboe II* and *Violino II*, with the alto; *Oboe da caccia* and *Viola*, with the tenor; and *Continuo*, with the bass.

Bach notates this in the signature of two flats, with a considerable use of the additional A♭. Terry presents the signature of three flats in his number 44. He also offers an original translation. Schirmer B-R; I, p. 110 uses an original translation by the author of these notes.

120. Was mein Gott will, das g'scheh' allzeit

This chorale closes Cantata 103, "Ihr werdet weinen und heulen", with the text of the ninth stanza of the hymn.

Ich hab' dich einen Augenblick,
o liebes Kind, verlassen;
sieh' aber, sieh' mit grossem Glück
und Trost ohn' alle Maassen:

will ich dir schon die Freuden-Kron'
aufsetzen und verehren.
Dein kurzes Leid
soll sich in Freud'
und ewig Wohl verkehren.

Terry, no. 361, offers his own translation.

Tromba, Flauto traverso, Oboi d'amore I & II, and *Violino I* play with the soprano; *Violino II,* with the alto; *Viola,* with the tenor; and *Continuo,* with the bass.

An identical harmonization of this chorale is found as No. 349 in this edition, under the name of "Ich hab' in Gottes Herz und Sinn".

121. Werde munter, mein Gemüte

This chorale, with the sixth stanza of the hymn, is found in the second part of the "St. Matthew Passion".

> *Bin ich gleich von dir gewichen,*
> *stell' ich mich doch wieder ein;*
> *Hat uns doch dein Sohn verglichen*
> *durch sein' Angst und Todespein.*
> *Ich verleugne nicht die Schuld,*
> *aber deine Gnad' und Huld*
> *ist viel grösser als die Sünde,*
> *die ich stets in mir befinde.*

Schirmer B-R, I, p. 127, offers an English translation by Dr. Emanuel Cronenwett. Terry, no. 384, uses one by Catherine Winkworth.

Flauti traversi I & II, Oboi I & II, and *Violino I* play with the soprano; *Violino II,* with the alto; *Viola,* with the tenor; and *Organo* and *Continuo,* with the bass.

122. Ist Gott mein Schild und Helfersmann

This chorale concludes Cantata 85, "Ich bin ein guter Hirt", with the fourth stanza:

> *Ist Gott mein Schutz und treuer Hirt,*
> *kein Unglück mich berühren wird;*
> *weicht, alle meine Feinde,*
> *die ihr mir stiftet Angst und Pein,*
> *es wird zu eurem Schaden sein;*
> *ich habe Gott zum Freunde,*
> *ich habe Gott zum Freunde.*

Schirmer B-R, I, p. 114, offers an English translation by Dr. Charles N. Boyd. Terry, no. 197, presents his own translation.

Oboi I & II and *Violino I* play with the soprano; *Violino II,* with the alto; *Viola,* with the tenor; and *Continuo,* with the bass.

123. Helft mir Gott's Güte preisen

This chorale is placed at the end of Cantata 183, "Sie werden euch in den Bann thun", where it makes use of the fifth stanza:

> *Du bist ein Geist, der lehret,*
> *wie man recht beten soll;*
> *dein Beten wird erhöret,*
> *dein Singen klinget wohl;*
> *es steigt zum Himmel an,*
> *es steigt und lässt nicht abe,*
> *bis der geholfen habe,*
> *der allein helfen kann.*

Terry, no. 130, presents his own translation.

Oboi d'amore I & II and *Violino I* play with the soprano; *Oboe da caccia I* and *Violino II,* with the alto; *Oboe da caccia II* and *Viola,* with the tenor; and *Continuo,* with the bass.

124. Auf, auf, mein Herz, und du mein ganzer Sinn (n.s.)

125. Allein Gott in der Höh' sei Ehr'

This is possibly an altered version of the closing number of Cantata 104, "Du Hirte Israel, höre", where it appears with the first stanza of "Der Herr ist mein getreuer Hirt". There is also a possibility of its being a number from a lost cantata, since it appears here in the key of G major and in Cantata 104 in the key of A major. The measure before the last has also been changed both in the melody and in the harmonization. The harmonization, as it appears in the cantata, may be found in No. 326 of this edition; the words, as well as other details concerning the chorale, may also be found in the note on No. 326.

126. Durch Adams Fall ist ganz verderbt

This chorale was discussed under No. 100. It has here been transposed to A minor, but is otherwise the same.

127. Dies sind die heil'gen zehn Gebot' (n.s.)

128. Alles ist an Gottes Segen (n.s.)

The three low D's in the bass seem to have been taken from an instrumental bass.

129. Keinen hat Gott verlassen (n.s.)

130. Meine Seele erhebet den Herrn (n.s.)

131. Liebster Jesu, wir sind hier (n.s.)

132. Kyrie, Gott Vater in Ewigkeit (n.s.)

This may have been an arrangement of the *Kyrie* for a special church service; however, if it is from a larger work, that work has disappeared.

133. Wir glauben all' an einen Gott (n.s.)

134. Du, o schönes Weltgebäude (n.s.)

Attention is called to the details concerning No. 87, where the chorale was drawn from Cantata 56. The bass part in the measure-and-a-half following the repeat has the appearance of having been adapted from the instrumental bass.

135. Gott der Vater wohn' uns bei (n.s.)

136. Herr Jesu Christ, dich zu uns wend' (n.s.)

137. Wer Gott vertraut, hat wohl gebaut (n.s.)

138. Jesu, meine Freude

This chorale closes Cantata 64, "Sehet, welch' eine Liebe hat uns der Vater erzeiget", with the fifth stanza of the hymn.

> *Gute Nacht, o Wesen,*
> *das die Welt erlesen!*
> *mir gefällst du nicht.*
> *Gute Nacht, ihr Sünden,*
> *bleibet weit dahinten,*
> *kommt nicht mehr an's Licht!*
> *Gute Nacht, du Stolz und Pracht!*
> *dir sei ganz, o Lasterleben,*
> *gute Nacht gegeben!*

Terry, no. 214, offers his own translation.
Violino I and *Cornetta* play with the soprano;

Violino II and *Trombone I*, with the alto; *Viola* and *Trombone II*, with the tenor; and *Trombone III* and *Organo & Continuo* with the bass.

139. Warum sollt' ich mich denn grämen

This chorale has its place near the close of Part III of the "Christmas Oratorio", with the text of the fifteenth stanza of the hymn "Fröhlich soll mein Herze springen".

> *Ich will dich mit Fleiss bewahren,*
> *ich will dir leben hier,*
> *dir will ich abfahren.*
> *Mit dir will ich endlich schweben*
> *voller Freud',*
> *ohne Zeit*
> *dort im andern Leben.*

Schirmer B-R, I, p. 90, offers an English translation by Catherine Winkworth.
Flauti traversi I & II (in 8ᵗⁿ), *Oboi I & II*, and *Violino I* play with the soprano; *Violino II*, with the alto; *Viola*, with the tenor; and *Organo* and *Continuo*, with the bass.

140. In allen meinen Taten (n.s.)

141. Seelen-Bräutigam (n.s.)

142. Schwing' dich auf zu deinem Gott

Cantata 40, "Dazu ist erschienen der Sohn Gottes", contains three chorale harmonizations in the latter half of the work. The present chorale appears as the second one and is placed near the close of the cantata. The words are the second stanza of the hymn.

> *Schüttle deinen Kopf und sprich:*
> *fleuch, du alte Schlange!*
> *was erneurst du deinen Stich,*
> *machst mir angst und bange?*
> *Ist dir doch der Kopf zerknickt,*
> *und ich bin durch's Leiden*
> *meines Heilands dir entrückt*
> *in den Saal der Freuden.*

Schirmer B-R, I, p. 105, presents a translation by the author of these notes. Terry, no. 315, also presents an original translation.
Corno I, *Oboe I*, and *Violino I* play with the soprano; *Oboe II* and *Violino II*, with the alto;

Viola, with the tenor; and *Continuo*, with the bass.

143. In dulci Jubilo (n.s.)

144. Wer in dem Schutz des Höchsten (n.s.)

This chorale is usually known under the name "Herr, wie du willst, so schick's mit mir", and among the "371" No. 318 presents the identical harmonization under that name.

145. Warum betrübst du dich (n.s.)

Attention is called to the last few measures: evidently the bass part should be one octave higher for the vocal bass.

146. Wer nur den lieben Gott lässt walten (n.s.)

147. Wenn ich in Angst und Not (n.s.)

148. Uns ist ein Kindlein heut' gebor'n (n.s.)

This chorale is usually known under the name "Ach, bleib bei uns, Herr Jesu Christ". This same harmonization may be found under that name as No. 177. The only difference is that No. 177 appears in A major and without the repeat of the first five measures. This is to accommodate the music to the four-line stanza of "Ach, bleib bei uns, Herr Jesu Christ" instead of the six-line stanza of "Uns ist ein Kindlein heut' gebor'n".

149. Nicht so traurig, nicht so sehr (n.s.)

150. Welt, ade! ich bin dein müde

This harmonization is not by Bach, but by Johann Rosenmüller. It was published for the first time in Johann Quirsfeld's *Geistliche Harffen-Klang* (Leipzig, 1679). Bach made use of it to bring Cantata 27, "Wer weiss, wie nahe mir mein Ende", to a close with the following text:

Welt, ade! ich bin dein müde,
ich will nach dem Himmel zu,
da wird sein der rechte Friede
und die ew'ge, stolze Ruh.

Welt, bei dir ist Krieg und Streit,
nichts, denn lauter Eitelkeit;
in dem Himmel allezeit
Friede, Freud' und Seeligkeit.

Schirmer B-R, I, p. 126, uses the translation by Catherine Winkworth. Terry, no. 365, presents his own translation.

Corno and *Oboi I & II* play with soprano I; *Violino I*, with soprano II; *Violino II*, with the alto; *Viola*, with the tenor; and *Continuo*, with the bass.

The signature of one flat was used by Bach in the score.

151. Meinen Jesum lass' ich nicht, Jesus (n.s.)

152. Meinen Jesum lass' ich nicht, weil

This brings Cantata 154, "Mein liebster Jesus ist verloren", to a close with the sixth stanza:

Meinen Jesum lass' ich nicht,
geh' ihm ewig an der Seiten;
Christus lässt mich für und für
zu dem Lebensbächlein leiten.
Selig, der mit mir so spricht:
Meinen Jesum lass' ich nicht!

Terry, no. 252, presents his own translation.

The editor of the score of the Bachgesellschaft edition has indicated the instruments as follows: *Oboi I & II* and *Violino I* with the soprano; *Violino II* with the alto; *Viola* with the tenor; and *Continuo* with the bass. Other instruments used in the cantata are *Oboi d'amore I & II*.

153. Alle Menschen müssen sterben (n.s.)

154. Der du bist drei in Einigkeit (n.s.)

155. Hilf, Herr Jesu, lass gelingen (n.s.)

This melody is different from the one under the same name in No. 368, which is taken from the "Christmas Oratorio".

156. Ach Gott, wie manches Herzeleid

This chorale is the closing number of Cantata 3, "Ach Gott, wie manches Herzeleid", where it is used with the eighteenth stanza of the hymn.

Erhalt' mein Herz im Glauben rein,
so leb' und sterb' ich dir allein.
Jesu, mein Trost, hör' mein Begier':
o mein Heiland, wär' ich bei dir!

Schirmer B-R, I, p. 78, presents a translation by J. C. Jacobi.

Violino I, Corno, and *Oboi d'amore I & II* play with the soprano; *Violino II,* with the alto; *Viola,* with the tenor; and *Continuo,* with the bass.

157. Wo Gott zum Haus nicht gibt (n.s.)

158. Der Tag, der ist so freudenreich (n.s.)

159. Als der gütige Gott (n.s.)

160. Gelobet seist du, Jesu Christ

Cantata 64, "Sehet, welch' eine Liebe hat uns der Vater erzeiget", contains three chorales, of which this is the first in order of appearance. The seventh stanza is used:

Das hat er Alles uns gethan,
sein' gross' Lieb' zu zeigen an.
Dess freu' sich alle Christenheit
und dank' ihm dess in Ewigkeit.
Kyrie eleis!

Schirmer B-R, I, p. 82, uses a translation by Richard Massie. Terry, no. 112, presents his own translation.

Violino I and *Cornetto* play with the soprano; *Violino II* and *Trombone I,* with the alto; *Viola* and *Trombone II,* with the tenor; and *Trombone III, Organo,* and *Continuo,* with the bass.

161. Ihr Gestirn', ihr hohlen Lüfte (n.s.)

A free version of the melody may be found in the 69 Melodies from Schemelli's *Gesangbuch.*

162. Das alte Jahr vergangen ist (n.s.)

163. Für Freuden lasst uns springen (n.s.)

164. Herr Gott, dich loben alle wir (n.s.)

165. O Lamm Gottes, unschuldig (n.s.)

166. Es stehn vor Gottes Throne (n.s.)

167. Du grosser Schmerzensmann (n.s.)

168. Heut' ist, o Mensch, ein grosser (n.s.)

169. Jesu, der du selbsten wohl (n.s.)

170. Nun komm, der Heiden Heiland

This chorale, in its original key of B minor, brings to a close Cantata 62, "Nun komm, der Heiden Heiland", where it appears with the eighth stanza of the hymn. In the "371" it has been transposed to A minor.

Lob sei Gott, dem Vater, g'than,
Lob sei Gott, sein'm ein'gen Sohn,
Lob sei Gott, dem heil'gen Geist,
immer und in Ewigkeit.

Terry, no. 272, presents his own translation. Schirmer B-R, I, p. 88, presents a translation by the author of these notes.

Corno, Oboi I & II, and *Violino I* play with the soprano; *Violino II,* with the alto; *Viola,* with the tenor; and *Continuo,* with the bass.

171. Schaut, ihr Sünder (n.s.)

172. Sei gegrüsset, Jesu gütig (n.s.)

This is a realization of the melody by the same name contained in the 69 Melodies with figured bass in Schemelli's *Gesangbuch.* It is possible that this harmonization had its source in the group of 88 harmonized chorales that Bach made for his own use.

173. O Herzensangst (n.s.)

174. Jesus Christus, unser Heiland, der den Tod (n.s.)

Erk, no. 249, places the chorale one step higher. At least the low notes in the final measures seem to have been derived from the instrumental bass.

175. Jesus, meine Zuversicht (n.s.)

176. Erstanden ist der heil'ge Christ (n.s.)

177. Ach bleib bei uns, Herr Jesu Christ (n.s.)

For details concerning this chorale, please refer to No. 148, where it appears in the same harmonization but transposed to G major and with a repeat for the first five measures.

178. Das neugeborne Kindelein

For details, please see notes under No. 53.

179. Wachet auf, ruft uns die Stimme

This well-known and excellent chorale closes Cantata 140, "Wachet auf, ruft uns die Stimme", with the third stanza of the hymn.

> *Gloria sei dir gesungen*
> *mit Menschen- und englischen Zungen,*
> *mit Harfen und mit Cymbeln schon.*
> *Von zwölf Perlen sind die Pforten*
> *an deiner Stadt; wir sind Consorten*
> *der Engel hoch um deinen Thron.*
> *Kein Aug' hat je gespürt,*
> *kein Ohr hat je gehört*
> *solche Freude.*
> *Dess sind wir froh,*
> *io! io!*
> *ewig in dulci jubilo.*

Schirmer B-R, I, p. 107, offers an English translation by Dr. Emanuel Cronenwett. Terry, no. 342, uses his own translation.

Violino piccolo (in 8vo), Corno, Oboe I, and *Violino I* play with the soprano; *Oboe II* and *Violino II,* with the alto; *Taille* and *Viola,* with the tenor; and *Continuo,* with the bass.

180. Als Jesus Christus in der Nacht (n.s.)

Several of the low notes were probably derived from the instrumental bass.

181. Gott hat das Evangelium (n.s.)

182. Wär' Gott nicht mit uns diese Zeit

This chorale closes Cantata 14, "Wär' Gott nicht mit uns diese Zeit", with the third stanza of the hymn.

> *Gott Lob und Dank, der nicht zugab,*
> *dass ihr Schlund uns mögt fangen.*
> *Wie ein Vogel des Stricks kömmt ab,*
> *ist unsre Seel' entgangen.*
> *Strick ist entzwei und wir sind frei,*
> *des Herren Name steht uns bei,*
> *des Gottes Himmels und Erden.*

Schirmer B-R, I, p. 126, uses a translation by Richard Massie. Terry, no. 343, employs his own translation.

Corno di caccia, Oboi I & II, and *Violino I* play with the soprano; *Violino II,* with the alto; *Viola,* with the tenor; and *Continuo,* with the bass.

183. Nun freut euch, lieben Christen, g'mein (n.s.)

184. Christ lag in Todesbanden

This chorale closes Cantata 4, "Christ lag in Todesbanden", in which every movement is based upon the chorale melody. The stanza for this final chorale is the seventh:

> *Wir essen und leben wohl*
> *im rechten Osterfladen,*
> *der alte Sauerteig nicht soll*
> *sein bei dem Wort der Gnaden,*
> *Christus will die Koste sein*
> *und speisen die Seel' allein,*
> *der Glaub' will keins andern leben.*
> *Hallelujah!*

Schirmer B-R, I, p. 80, presents a translation by Dr. Charles N. Boyd. Terry, no. 39, uses his own translation.

Violini I & II and *Cornetto* play with the soprano; *Viola I* and *Trombone I,* with the alto; *Viola II* and *Trombone II,* with the tenor; and *Trombone III* and *Continuo,* with the bass.

The original is in the key of E minor; the version in the "371" is in D minor, without the signature of one flat.

185. Nun freut euch, Gottes Kinder all' (n.s.)

186. Ach Gott, erhör' mein Seufzen (n.s.)

The 1832 edition changed the alto on the last beat of the third measure and the first beat of the fourth measure from two quarter notes, each being A below middle C, to its form in this edition. Terry maintains that no reason exists for this change.

187. Komm, Gott Schöpfer, heiliger Geist (n.s.)

188. Ich dank' dir schon durch deinen Sohn
(n.s.)

189. Herr Jesu Christ, wahr'r Mensch und Gott (n.s.)

190. Herr, nun lass in Frieden (n.s.)

191. Von Gott will ich nicht lassen

This chorale forms the closing number of Cantata 73, "Herr, wie du willt, so schick's mit mir". The ninth stanza is used:

> *Das ist des Vaters Wille,*
> *der uns erschaffen hat;*
> *sein Sohn hat Gut's die Fülle*
> *erworben uns aus Gnad';*
> *auch Gott, der heil'ge Geist,*
> *im Glauben uns regieret,*
> *zum Reich des Himmels führet:*
> *ihm sei Lob, Ehr' und Preis.*

Schirmer B-R, I, p. 106, uses a translation from the Moravian Hymn Book of 1754. Terry, no. 341, uses the translation by Catherine Winkworth.

Corno, Oboe I, and *Violino I* play with the soprano; *Oboe II* and *Violino II*, with the alto; *Viola*, with the tenor; and *Continuo*, with the bass.

This chorale appears in the original in two flats, with a Dorian significance. In the present edition it is placed directly in the signature for A minor.

192. Gottlob, es geht nunmehr zu Ende
(n.s.)

193. Was bist du doch, o Seele, so betrübet
(n.s.)

This harmonization is a realization of the melody and figured bass as presented under number 55 of the group of 69 from the Schemelli *Gesangbuch*. It was probably taken from the collection of 88 which Bach is known to have made for his personal use.

194. Liebster Immanuel, Herzog der Frommen

This chorale is the closing number of Cantata 123, which bears the same name as the chorale. The stanza is the sixth:

> *Drum fahrt nur immerhin, ihr Eitelkeiten!*
> *Du, Jesu, du bist mein und ich bin dein;*
> *ich will mich von der Welt zu dir bereiten;*
> *du sollt in meinem Herz und Munde sein!*
> *Mein ganzes Leben*
> *sei dir ergeben,*
> *bis man mich einstens legt in's Grab hinein.*

Schirmer B-R, I, p. 86, presents a translation by the author of these notes. Terry, no. 234, uses his own translation.

Flauti traversi I & II (in 8ᵛᵃ), Oboi d'amore I & II, and *Violino I* play with the soprano; *Violino II*, with the alto; *Viola*, with the tenor; and *Continuo*, with the bass.

It should be noted that the soprano and alto cross on the second beat of the fourth measure after the repeat, the soprano melody proceeding from C♯ down to F♯ and then up to D.

195. Wie schön leuchtet der Morgenstern

This chorale was changed slightly in the ninth and tenth measures in the edition published in 1831. It is an exact duplication of Nos. 86 and 305, making three duplicate harmonizations of the same chorale among the "371".

196. Da der Herr Christ zu Tische sass (n.s.)

197. Christ ist erstanden (n.s.)

This is evidently a three-stanza harmonization prepared for the church service. It is extremely interesting to note how Bach varied the harmonization for each stanza: a counterpart, in the idiom of the organ, exists in the *Orgelbüchlein*, where the three stanzas are also completely worked out.

198. Christus, der uns selig macht (n.s.)

This number is identical with No. 307, except for the manner of writing a few tied notes. There can be no doubt that some of the bass part must have been derived from the instrumental bass.

199. Hilf, Gott, dass mir's gelinge (n.s.)

This is an exact duplicate of No. 302.

**200. Christus ist erstanden, hat über-
wunden** (n.s.)

201. O Mensch, bewein' dein' Sünde gross
(n.s.)

Except for minor differences of notation, this
number is a duplicate of No. 306.

202. O wir armen Sünder (n.s.)

203. O Mensch, schau Jesum Christum an
(n.s.)

204. Wer weiss, wie nahe mir

This chorale is more usually known under the
name of "Wer nur den lieben Gott lässt walten".
This harmonization brings to a conclusion Cantata 166, "Wo gehest du hin?" The first stanza
of the hymn "Wer weiss, wie nahe mir mein
Ende" is used (hence the name that stands in
the "371" as the title of this number).

> *Wer weiss, wie nahe mir mein Ende,*
> *hin geht die Zeit, her kommt der Tod.*
> *Ach, wie geschwinde und behende*
> *kann kommen meine Todesnoth!*
> *Mein Gott, ich bitt' durch Christi Blut:*
> *mach's nur mit meinem Ende gut!*

Terry, no. 376, offers his own translation.
Oboe and *Violino I* play with the soprano;
Violino II, with the alto; *Viola*, with the tenor;
and *Continuo*, with the bass.

205. Herr Gott, dich loben wir (n.s.)

This setting of the *Te Deum* seems to be a
practical arrangement for use in the church
service. It is possible that it may have been
derived from the selection of 88 harmonizations
that Bach is known to have made for himself.
He made another similar arrangement of this
chorale which may be found published among the
miscellaneous group of chorale preludes for the
organ.

**206. So gibst du nun, mein Jesu, gute
Nacht** (n.s.)

With the exception of a few slight changes in
the bass, this harmonization is a realization of
the melody and bass of number 26 in the Schemelli group. It is possibly one of the 88 compiled by Bach. In the original 1786 edition the
eighth measure was omitted. This was corrected
in the 1831 edition.

207. Des heil'gen Geistes reiche Gnad' (n.s.)

Erk, deciding that the chorale had been transposed along with numerous others, presents it
in E minor. Smend, in his revision of Erk's
work, returns to the key of D minor.

208. Als vierzig Tag' nach Ostern (n.s.)

The melody bears a close resemblance to the
melody "Erschienen ist der herrlich' Tag".

209. Dir, dir, Jehovah, will ich singen

The source of this harmonization is the *Noten-
büchlein für Anna Magdalena Bach* (1725), where
are presented eight stanzas of the hymn, of
which the first is as follows:

> *Dir, dir, Jehovah, will ich singen:*
> *denn, wo ist so ein solcher Gott, wie du?*
> *Dir will ich meine Lieder bringen:*
> *ach! gieb mir deines Geistes Kraft darzu,*
> *dass ich es thu' im Namen Jesu Christ,*
> *so wie es dir durch ihn gefällig ist.*

**210. Christe, du Beistand deiner Kreuzge-
meine** (n.s.)

211. Weltlich Ehr' und zeitlich Gut (n.s.)

212. Herr, ich denk' an jene Zeit (n.s.)

**213. O wie selig seid ihr doch, ihr From-
men** (n.s.)

This harmonization is a realization of the
melody and figured bass that appears as number
65 of the Schemelli group. Students may gain
much benefit by studying Bach's manner of
realizing a figured bass and melody by comparing the two versions.

214. Mitten wir im Leben sind (n.s.)

215.   Verleih' uns Frieden gnädiglich

This harmonization is one of those that have undergone transposition in the preparation of the "371". Here it is in G minor, while in the key of A minor it forms the concluding number of Cantata 126, "Erhalt' uns, Herr, bei deinem Wort". It appears with the following stanza as the text:

> Verleih' uns Frieden gnädiglich,
> Herr Gott, zu unsern Zeiten;
> es ist ja doch kein And'rer nicht,
> der für uns könnte streiten,
> denn du, unser Gott, alleine.
> Gieb unserm Fürst'n und aller Obrigkeit
> Fried' und gut Regiment,
> dass wir unter ihnen
> ein geruh'g und stilles Leben führen mögen
> in aller Gottseligkeit und Ehrbarkeit.   Amen.

Terry, no. 333, uses his own translation. A translation by the author of these notes will be found in Schirmer B-R, I, p. 125, where the harmonization used, however, is the one from Cantata 42.

Tromba, Oboi I & II, and *Violino I* play with the soprano; *Violino II,* with the alto; *Viola,* with the tenor; and *Continuo,* with the bass.

216.   Es ist genug; so nimm, Herr

This number brings to a close Cantata 60, "O Ewigkeit, du Donnerwort", where it appears with the fifth stanza of the hymn.

> Es ist genug: Herr, wenn es dir gefällt,
> so spanne mich doch aus.
> Mein Jesus kommt: nun gute Nacht, o Welt!
> ich fahr' in's Himmelshaus,
> ich fahre sicher hin mit Frieden,
> mein grosser Jammer bleibt darnieden.
> Es ist genug, es ist genug.

Schirmer B-R, I, p. 96, presents a translation by Dr. Charles N. Boyd. Terry, no. 94, also offers his own translation.

Corno, Oboe d'amore I, and *Violino I* play with the soprano; *Oboe d'amore II* and *Violino II,* with the alto; *Viola,* with the tenor; and *Continuo,* with the bass.

217.   Ach Gott, wie manches Herzeleid

This harmonization closes Cantata 153, "Schau' lieber Gott, wie meine Feind'", with the following three stanzas of the hymn:

I. *Drum will ich, weil ich lebe noch,*
    das Kreuz dir fröhlich tragen nach;
    mein Gott mach' mich darzu bereit,
    es dient zum Besten allezeit!

II. *Hilf mir mein' Sach' recht greifen an,*
    dass ich mein' Lauf vollenden kann,
    hilf mir auch zwingen Fleisch und Blut,
    für Sünd' und Schanden mich behüt'!

III. *Erhalt' mein Herz im Glauben rein,*
    so leb' und sterb' ich dir allein;
    Jesu, mein Trost, hör' mein Begier,
    o mein Heiland, wär' ich bei dir!

For Bach to use three stanzas of a hymn for a chorale harmonization was most unusual. Terry, in his number 10, does not use these stanzas at all, but presents the first, second, third, twelfth, and fourteenth stanzas of the hymn "O Jesu Christ, meins Lebens Licht". In his book *Joh. Seb. Bach's Cantata Texts* he offers his translations of those presented above.

Violino I, Violino II, Viola, and *Continuo* play with the soprano, alto, tenor, and bass, respectively.

218.   Lass, o Herr, dein Ohr sich neigen (n.s.)

219.   O wie selig seid ihr doch, ihr Frommen (n.s.)

220.   Sollt' ich meinem Gott nicht singen (n.s.)

The melody of this chorale, together with a completely figured bass, is found as number 18 of the Schemelli group. With some slight freedom in the use of the figures, it is a realization of that melody and its bass. In the Schemelli group it is called "Lasset uns mit Jesu ziehen".

221.   Herr, straf mich nicht in deinem Zorn (n.s.)

222.   Nun preiset alle (n.s.)

223.   Ich dank' dir, Gott, für all' Wohltat (n.s.)

It is curious to note that Erk, no. 237, presents the harmonization a minor third higher, under the impression that it had been transposed by the copyist. Smend, in his revision, returns to the original key.

224. Das walt' Gott Vater und Gott Sohn (n.s.)

225. Gott, der du selber bist das Licht (n.s)

226. Herr Jesu Christ, du hast bereit (n.s.)

227. Lobet den Herren, denn er ist sehr freundlich (n.s.)

228. Danket dem Herren, denn er ist sehr freundlich (n.s.)

229. Ich danke dir, o Gott, in deinem Throne (n. s.)

230. Christ, der du bist der helle Tag (n.s.)

231. Die Nacht ist kommen (n.s.)

232. Die Sonn' hat sich mit ihrem Glanz (n.s.)

233. Werde munter, mein Gemüte

This harmonization appears as the third number of Cantata 154, "Mein liebster Jesus ist verloren". The second stanza of "Jesu meiner Seelen Wonne", under which name the chorale is often designated, is the one used.

Jesu, mein Hort und Erretter,
Jesu, meine Zuversicht,
Jesu, starker Schlangentreter,
Jesu, meines Lebens Licht!
Wie verlanget meinem Herzen,
Jesulein, nach dir mit Schmerzen!
Komm', ach komm', ich warte dein,
komm', o liebstes Jesulein!

Terry, no. 385, presents his own translation.

Since the existing autograph score is incomplete, the editor of this cantata in the Bach-gesellschaft edition suggests the instruments to be used. They are *Oboi I & II* and *Violino I*

with the soprano; *Violino II* with the alto; *Viola* with the tenor; and *Continuo* with the bass. This suggestion is in accordance with the usual distribution of the instruments for a chorale.

234. Gott lebet noch (n.s.)

This harmonization is a realization of the melody and figured bass presented as number 36 in the Schemelli group. It is possible that all of this type were derived by the copyist from the collection of 88 harmonizations which Bach was known to have made for his own use.

235. Heilig, heilig (n.s.)

This is a setting of the *Sanctus*, probably made for church use, and may have had its origin in the collection of 88 mentioned under the previous number. In No. 319 will be found an identical harmonization, under the name "Sanctus, Sanctus, Dominus Deus Sabaoth".

236. O Jesu, du mein Bräutigam (n.s.)

This melody is more correctly known under the name "O Jesu Christ, mein's Lebens Licht" or "Herr Jesu Christ, mein's Lebens Licht". An exact duplication of this harmonization is found as No. 295, with the latter title.

237. Was betrübst du dich, mein Herze (n.s.)

Some of the low notes are no doubt derived from the instrumental bass.

238. Es wird schier der letzte Tag (n.s.)

239. Den Vater dort oben (n.s.)

240. Nun sich der Tag geendet hat (n.s.)

241. Was willst du dich, o meine Seele (n.s.)

242. Wie bist du, Seele (n.s.)

243. Jesu, du mein liebstes Leben (n.s.)

244. Jesu, Jesu, du bist mein (n.s.)

This is a realization of the melody and figured bass presented as number 53 in the Schemelli group of 69.

245. Christe, der du bist Tag und Licht (n.s.)

246. Singt dem Herrn ein neues Lied (n.s.)

247. Wenn wir in höchsten Nöten sein (n.s.)

248. Sei Lob und Ehr' dem höchsten Gut

This chorale is more often known under the name "Es ist das Heil uns kommen her". The present harmonization is placed in the middle part of Cantata 117, "Sei Lob und Ehr' dem höchsten Gut", where it uses the fourth stanza of the hymn, together with directions that the same harmonization be sung at the close of the cantata with stanza nine:

IV. *Ich rief dem Herrn in meiner Noth:*
Ach Gott, vernimm mein Schreien!
Da half mein Helfer mir vom Tod
und liess mir Trost gedeihen.
Drum dank', ach Gott, drum dank' ich
    dir;
ach danket, danket Gott mit mir!
Gebt unserm Gott die Ehre!

(For the close of the cantata)
IX. *So kommet vor sein Angesicht*
mit jauchzenvollem Springen;
bezahlet die gelobte Pflicht,
und lasst uns fröhlich singen:
Gott hat es Alles wohl bedacht
und Alles, Alles wohl gemacht!
Gebt unserm Gott die Ehre!

In connection with this harmonization Terry, no. 93, gives his own translations of stanzas I, VII, and IX; and, in connection with another harmonization (his no. 92), he gives his own translations of stanzas I, III, and IV.

No indications are marked for the instruments to be used. Those used for the cantata are *Flauti traversi I & II, Oboi I & II, Oboi d'amore I & II*, Strings, and *Continuo*.

249. Allein Gott in der Höh' sei Ehr' (n.s.)

250. Ein' feste Burg ist unser Gott (n.s.)

251. Ich bin ja, Herr, in deiner Macht (n.s.)

252. Jesu, nun sei gepreiset (n.s.)

253. Ach Gott, vom Himmel sieh' darein (n.s.)

254. Weg, mein Herz, mit den Gedanken

This chorale, usually known under the name "Freu' dich sehr, O meine Seele", brings to a close Cantata 25, "Es ist nichts Gesundes an meinem Leibe". The stanza used is the twelfth:

Ich will alle meine Tage
rühmen deine starke Hand,
dass du meine Plag' und Klage
hast so herzlich abgewandt.
Nicht nur in der Sterblichkeit
soll dein Ruhm sein ausgebreit't:
ich will's auch hernach erweisen,
und dort ewiglich dich preisen.

Terry gives his own translation in his number 109.

The instrumentation is unusual: *Flauti I, II, & III, Oboe I, Cornetto*, and *Violino I* play with the soprano; *Oboe II, Trombone I*, and *Violino II*, with the alto; *Trombone II* and *Viola*, with the tenor; and *Trombone III* and *Continuo*, with the bass.

255. Was frag' ich nach der Welt

This chorale is more familiar under the name "O Gott, du frommer Gott". It occupies the middle part of Cantata 64, "Sehet, welch' eine Liebe hat uns der Vater erzeiget". The text is as follows:

Was frag' ich nach der Welt
und allen ihren Schätzen,
wenn ich mich nur an dir,
mein Jesu, kann ergötzen?
Dich hab' ich einzig mir
zur Wollust vorgestellt:
Du, du bist meine Lust;
was frag' ich nach der Welt!

Violino I and *Cornetto* play with the soprano; *Violino II* and *Trombone I*, with the alto; *Viola* and *Trombone II*, with the tenor; and *Trombone III*, *Organ* and *Continuo*, with the bass. The instrumental bass, which is not given in the reduction of this chorale for the "371", is elaborated more than usual and continues its sequence of eighth notes uninterruptedly from first to last, except during the three final beats. Terry, no. 285, presents the instrumental bass and also his own translation.

256. Jesu, deine tiefen Wunden

This chorale will be more readily recognized under the title "Freu' dich sehr, o meine Seele". Under No. 64 is found an identical harmonization, except that it appears in the key of G. In the key of B♭ it forms the closing number of the cantata "Höchsterwünschtes Freudenfest". For details concerning this setting, please refer to the notes under No. 64 in this book.

257. Nun lasst uns Gott, dem Herren

This harmonization is the same as No. 93, where it appears under the name "Wach auf, mein Herz".

258. Meine Augen schliess' ich jetzt (n.s.)

259. Verleih' uns Frieden gnädiglich

This harmonization is identical with that under No. 91.

260. Es ist gewisslich an der Zeit (n.s.)

This chorale is more frequently known under the name "Nun freut euch, lieben Christen g'mein".

261. Christ lag in Todesbanden (n.s.)

262. Ach Gott, vom Himmel sieh' darein

This harmonization, with the text of the sixth stanza, brings to a close Cantata 2, "Ach Gott, vom Himmel sieh' darein".

> *Das wollst du Gott bewahren rein*
> *für diesem arg'n Geschlechte,*
> *und lass uns dir befohlen sein,*

> *dass sich's in uns nicht flechte,*
> *der gottlos' Hauf' sich umher find't,*
> *wo solche lose Leute sind*
> *in deinem Volk erhaben.*

Terry, no. 6, presents the English translation by George Macdonald.

Violino I, Oboi I & II, and *Trombone I* play with the soprano; *Violino II* and *Trombone II*, with the alto; *Viola* and *Trombone III*, with the tenor; and *Trombone IV* and *Continuo*, with the bass.

263. Jesu, meine Freude

This harmonization serves as both the opening and closing number of the motet, "Jesu, meine Freude". Every alternate number of the motet is built upon this melody. Of the five harmonizations that the motet thus contains, this one is the simplest. The stanzas used are the first and the sixth.

> I. *Jesu, meine Freude,*
> *meines Herzens Weide,*
> *Jesu, meine Zier,*
> *ach, wie lang', ach, lange*
> *ist dem Herzen bange,*
> *und verlangt nach dir!*
> *Gottes Lamm,*
> *mein Bräutigam,*
> *ausser dir soll mir auf Erden*
> *nichts sonst Liebers werden.*

> VI. *Weicht, ihr Trauergeister,*
> *denn mein Freudenmeister,*
> *Jesus, tritt herein.*
> *Denen, die Gott lieben,*
> *muss auch ihr Betrüben*
> *lauter Zucker sein.*
> *Duld' ich schon hier Spott und Hohn,*
> *dennoch bleibst du auch im Leide,*
> *Jesu, meine Freude.*

Schirmer B-R, I, pp. 114f and 121, uses the translation by Catherine Winkworth. Terry, no. 210, offers his own translations for both stanzas.

No instrumentation was used for this motet, but authorities have concluded that Bach used the *Cembalo* (harpsichord) for accompanying motets in the church service.

264.   Jesu, meines Herzens Freud' (n.s.)

265.   Was mein Gott will, das

This work brings Cantata 144, "Nimm, was dein ist, und gehe hin", to a close with the text of the first stanza:

> *Was mein Gott will, das g'scheh' allzeit,*
> *sein Wille ist der beste.*
> *Zu helfen den'n er ist bereit,*
> *die an ihn glauben feste.*
> *Er hilft aus Noth,*
> *der fromme Gott,*
> *und züchtiget mit Maassen.*
> *Wer Gott vertraut,*
> *fest auf ihn baut,*
> *den wird er nicht verlassen.*

Schirmer B-R, I, p. 108, presents a translation by Dr. Charles N. Boyd; the harmonization, however, is a different one. Terry, no. 363, uses an original translation.

No indications show which instruments were used with the chorale. Strings, *Continuo*, and *Oboe d'amore* are indicated for the cantata. From many parallel cases, the use of the *Oboe d'amore* would indicate that at least one Oboe was used in the chorus parts, and perhaps two.

266.   Herr Jesu Christ, du höchstes Gut

This harmonization is the last number of Cantata 48, "Ich elender Mensch, wer wird mich erlösen". It uses the twelfth stanza as the text.

> *Herr Jesu Christ, einiger Trost,*
> *zu dir will ich mich wenden;*
> *mein Herzleid ist dir wohl bewusst,*
> *du kannst und wirst es enden.*
> *In deinen Willen sei's gestellt,*
> *mach's, lieber Gott, wie dir's gefällt:*
> *dein bin und will ich bleiben.*

Schirmer B-R, I, p. 98, uses a translation by Dr. Charles N. Boyd. Terry, no. 145, employs his own translation.

Tromba, Oboi I & II, and *Violino I* play with the soprano; *Violino II*, with the alto; *Viola*, with the tenor; and *Continuo*, with the bass.

267.   Vater unser im Himmelreich

The source of this harmonization is Cantata 90, "Es reifet euch ein schrecklich Ende", where it closes the cantata with the seventh stanza:

> *Leit' uns mit deiner rechten Hand,*
> *und segne unser' Stadt und Land:*
> *gieb uns allzeit dein heil'ges Wort,*
> *behüt' vor Teufel's List und Mord,*
> *verleih' ein sel'ges Stündelein,*
> *auf dass wir ewig bei dir sein!*

Terry, no. 331, provides his own translation.

No directions for the instruments were contained in the manuscript score by Bach.

268.   Nun lob', mein' Seel', den Herren (n.s.)

269.   Jesu, der du meine Seele (n.s.)

270.   Befiehl du deine Wege

This melody is the well-known "Herzlich thut mich verlangen". In this harmonization it closes Cantata 161, "Komm, du süsse Todesstunde", with the fourth stanza of the hymn.

> *Der Leib zwar in der Erden*
> *von Würmern wird verzehrt,*
> *doch auferweckt soll werden,*
> *durch Christum schön verklärt,*
> *wird leuchten als die Sonne*
> *und leben ohne Noth*
> *in himml'scher Freud' und Wonne.*
> *Was schad't mir dann der Tod?*

Violino I, Violino II, Viola, and *Continuo* appear on separate staves, duplicating the soprano, alto, tenor, and bass parts, respectively. The whole is crowned by an obbligato for flute, written on two staves for *Flauto I* and *Flauto II*. The aesthetic picture produced by this lively flute part suggests the awakening and resurrection of the body as expressed in the words of the stanza.

The complete and correct form, together with a translation by Dr. Charles N. Boyd, is presented as number 96 in Schirmer B-R, book II. Terry, no. 158, presents his own translation.

271.   Gib dich zufrieden und sei stille (n.s.)

272.   Ich dank' dir, lieber Herre (n.s.)

273.   Ein' feste Burg ist unser Gott

This well-known Reformation chorale ends the cantata written for the Reformation Sunday,

Cantata 80, "Ein' feste Burg ist unser Gott".
The stanza used was the fourth:

Das Wort sie sollen lassen stahn
und kein'n Dank dazu haben.
Er ist bei uns wohl auf dem Plan
mit seinem Geist und Gaben.
Nehmen sie uns den Leib,
Gut, Ehr', Kind und Weib,
lass fahren dahin;
sie haben's kein'n Gewinn;
das Reich muss uns doch bleiben.

Schirmer B-R, I, p. 94, uses the English translation by Catherine Winkworth. Terry, no. 79, presents his own translation.

The instruments for the chorale are not indicated in the score, but no doubt all of those employed in the cantata were used. They are as follows: *Tromba I, II, & III, Timpani, Oboi I & II, Oboi d'amore I & II, Taille, Oboe da caccia,* Strings, and *Organo.*

274. O Ewigkeit, du Donnerwort

This harmonization is a realization of the melody and bass appearing as the closing number in the Notebook for Anna Magdalena Bach.

275. O Welt, sieh hier dein Leben (n.s.)

The name under which this melody is known is "O Welt, ich muss dich lassen".

276. Lobt Gott, ihr Christen, allzugleich (n.s.)

277. Herzlich lieb hab' ich dich, o Herr (n.s.)

278. Wie schön leuchtet der Morgenstern (n.s.)

279. Ach Gott und Herr

This harmonization occupies a place approximately in the middle of Cantata 48, "Ich elender Mensch, wer wird mich erlösen". The text is the fourth stanza:

Soll's ja so sein, dass Straf' und Pein
auf Sünden folgen müssen:
so fahr' hier fort und schone dort,
und lass mich hier wohl büssen.

Schirmer B-R, I, p. 91, uses the English translation by Catherine Winkworth.

Tromba, Oboi I & II, and *Violino I* play with the soprano; *Violino II,* with the alto; *Viola,* with the tenor; and *Continuo,* with the bass.

280. Eins ist not! ach Herr, dies Eine (n.s.)

281. Wo soll ich fliehen hin

The more usual name for this melody is "Auf meinen lieben Gott". This version is found at the close of Cantata 89, "Was soll ich aus dir machen, Ephraim?" together with the text of the seventh stanza:

Mir mangelt zwar sehr viel,
doch, was ich haben will,
ist Alles, mir zu gute,
erlangt mit deinem Blute,
damit ich überwinde
Tod, Teufel, Höll' und Sünde.

Oboi I & II, Corno, and *Violino I* play with the soprano; *Violino II,* with the alto; *Viola,* with the tenor; and *Continuo,* with the bass. Terry, in his number 27, presents an original translation.

282. Freu' dich sehr, o meine Seele

The details concerning this harmonization may be found by consulting the notes in number 254 of this book. The identical harmonization occurs there under the name "Weg, mein Herz, mit den Gedanken".

283. Jesu, meine Freude

This is the seventh of eleven numbers comprising the motet "Jesu, meine Freude". Every alternate number of this motet is built upon the melody of this beautiful chorale. The stanza is the fourth:

Weg mit allen Schätzen,
du bist mein Ergötzen,
Jesu, meine Lust!
Weg, ihr eitlen Ehren,
ich mag euch nicht hören,
bleibt mir unbewusst!
Elend, Noth, Kreuz, Schmach und Tod
soll mich, ob ich viel muss leiden,
nicht von Jesu scheiden.

Schirmer B-R, I, p. 116, uses the English translation by Catherine Winkworth. Terry, no. 213, offers his own translation.

No instruments are designated since the motets were usually supported by the harpsichord or organ alone.

284.   Herr Jesu Christ, wahr'r Mensch und Gott

This harmonization brings to a close Cantata 127, "Herr Jesu Christ, wahr'r Mensch und Gott". The eighth stanza of the hymn is used as the text.

> *Ach Herr, vergieb all' unsre Schuld,*
> *hilf, dass wir warten mit Geduld,*
> *bis unser Stündlein kömmt herbei,*
> *auch unser Glaub' stets wacker sei,*
> *dein'm Wort zu trauen festiglich,*
> *bis wir einschlafen seliglich.*

Schirmer B-R, I, p. 99, uses an English translation by Dr. Emanuel Cronenwett. Terry, no. 149, presents his own translation.

Flauti I & II (in 8ᵛᵃ), *Oboi I & II*, and *Violino I* play with the soprano; *Violino II*, with the alto; *Viola*, with the tenor; and *Continuo*, with the bass.

Another melody under the same name, but four measures shorter, is found as No. 189 of this set.

285.   Wär' Gott nicht mit uns diese Zeit (n.s.)

The tune commonly known under this name is a different one. The present one will be recognized under the name "Wo Gott der Herr nicht bei uns hält".

286.   Befiehl du deine Wege (n.s.)

The more usual name for this melody is "Herzlich thut mich verlangen".

287.   Herr, ich habe missgehandelt (n.s.)

288.   Gelobet seist du, Jesu Christ (n.s.)

289.   Nun ruhen alle Wälder (n.s.)

This melody is commonly known as "O Welt ich muss dich lassen".

290.   Es ist das Heil uns kommen her

This harmonization forms the close of **Cantata 9**, "Es ist das Heil uns kommen her". **The** stanza used is the twelfth:

> *Ob sich's anliess, als wollt' er nicht,*
> *lass dich es nicht erschrecken,*
> *denn wo er ist am besten mit,*
> *da will er's nicht entdecken;*
> *sein Wort lass dir gewisser sein,*
> *und ob dein Herz spräch lauter Nein,*
> *so lass doch dir nicht grauen.*

Terry, no. 90, presents his own English translation.

Flauto traverso (in 8ᵛᵃ), *Oboe d'amore*, **and** *Violino I* play with the soprano; *Violino II*, with the alto; *Viola*, with the tenor; and *Continuo*, with the bass.

291.   Was frag' ich nach der Welt

This is usually known as one of the melodies under the name of "O Gott, du frommer Gott". It brings to a close **Cantata 94**, "Was frag ich nach der Welt". The harmonization makes use of two stanzas of the hymn, the seventh and the eighth.

> VII.   *Was frag ich nach der Welt!*
> *im Hui muss sie verschwinden,*
> *ihr Ansehn kann durchaus*
> *den blassen Tod nicht binden.*
> *Die Güter müssen fort,*
> *und alle Lust verfällt;*
> *bleibt Jesus nur bei mir:*
> *was frag ich nach der Welt!*

> VIII.   *Was frag ich nach der Welt!*
> *mein Jesus ist mein Leben,*
> *mein Schatz, mein Eigenthum,*
> *dem ich mich ganz ergeben,*
> *mein ganzes Himmelreich,*
> *und was mir sonst gefällt.*
> *Drum sag ich noch einmal:*
> *was frag ich nach der Welt!*

Terry, no. 286, offers his own translation.

Flauto traverso (in 8ᵛᵃ), *Oboe I*, and *Violino I* play with the soprano; *Oboe II* and *Violino II*, with the alto; *Viola*, with the tenor; and *Organo* and *Continuo*, with the bass.

The same harmonization was also used, it seems, as an alternate for a more elaborate harmonization in Cantata 64, "Sehet welch' eine Liebe". The text used in the latter was the first stanza.

292. Nimm von uns, Herr, du treuer Gott

This melody is known under the name "Vater unser im Himmelreich". This harmonization brings to a close Cantata 101, "Nimm von uns, Herr, du treuer Gott", where it is used with the words of the seventh stanza:

> Leit' uns mit deiner rechten Hand
> und segne unsre Stadt und Land;
> gieb uns allzeit dein heil'ges Wort,
> behüt' vor's Teufels List und Mord,
> verleih' ein sel'ges Stündelein,
> auf dass wir ewig bei dir sei'n!

Terry, no. 329, offers his own translation.

Flauto traverso (in 8°°), *Oboe I, Cornetto,* and *Violino I* play with the soprano; *Oboe II, Trombone I,* and *Violino II,* with the alto; *Taille, Trombone II,* and *Viola,* with the tenor; and *Trombone III* and *Continuo,* with the bass. Frequently the *Oboe II* diverges from the course of the alto part. This is also the case with the *Taille* and the tenor part.

293. Was Gott tut, das ist wohlgetan

This harmonization formed the close of the first version of Cantata 69, "Lobe den Herrn, meine Seele". It is also to be found in the second addendum to volume XVI of the Bachgesellschaft edition. The stanza is the sixth:

> Was Gott thut, das ist wohlgethan,
> dabei will ich verbleiben.
> Es mag mich auf die rauhe Bahn
> Noth, Tod und Elend treiben:
> so wird Gott mich ganz väterlich
> in seinen Armen halten.
> Drum lass ich ihn nur walten.

Terry, no 353, presents his own translation.

Tromba I, Oboi I & II, and *Violino I* play with the soprano; *Oboe III* and *Violino II,* with the alto; *Viola,* with the tenor; and *Fagotto* and *Continuo,* with the bass. The *Viola* deviates several times from the line of the tenor voice.

A very similar harmonization, in the key of B♭, is used in Cantata 12, "Weinen, Klagen, Sorgen, Zagen". In the latter case it has an elaborate obbligato, to be played by Oboe or Trumpet.

294. Herr Jesu Christ, du höchstes Gut

This forms the concluding number of Cantata 113, "Herr Jesu Christ, du höchstes Gut". The text is the eighth stanza.

> Stärk' mich mit deinem Freudengeist,
> heil' mich mit deinen Wunden;
> wasch' mich mit deinem Todesschweiss
> in meiner letzten Stunden;
> und nimm mich einst, wann dir's gefällt,
> im wahren Glauben von der Welt
> zu deinen Auserwählten.

Terry, no. 146, presents his own translation.

The instruments are not indicated for the chorale. Those used in the cantata are *Oboi I & II, Flauto traverso,* Strings, and *Continuo.*

295. Herr Jesu Christ, mein's Lebens Licht (n.s.)

Almost the identical harmonization was noted as No. 236 under the name "O Jesu, du mein Bräutigam".

296. Nun lob', mein' Seel', den Herren (n.s.)

297. Jesu, der du meine Seele

This harmonization concludes Cantata 78, "Jesu, der du meine Seele". The stanza used is the twelfth:

> Herr! ich glaube, hilf mir Schwachen,
> lass mich ja verzagen nicht;
> du, du kannst mich stärker machen,
> wenn mich Sünd' und Tod anficht.
> Deiner Güte will ich trauen,
> bis ich fröhlich werde schauen
> dich, Herr Jesu, nach dem Streit
> in der süssen Ewigkeit.

Schirmer B-R, I, p. 100, offers a translation by Dr. Charles N. Boyd. Terry, no. 199, offers his own translation.

Flauto traverso (*in 8ᵛᵃ*), *Oboe I*, *Corno*, and *Violino I* play with the soprano; *Oboe II* and *Violino II*, with the alto; *Viola*, with the tenor; and *Continuo*, with the bass.

298. Weg, mein Herz, mit den Gedanken

This chorale is better known under the name "Freu dich sehr, o meine Seele". It closes in festal manner Cantata 19, "Es erhub sich ein Streit". The stanza is the ninth:

> *Lass dein' Engel mit mir fahren*
> *auf Elias Wagen roth,*
> *und mein' Seele wohl bewahren,*
> *wie Laz'rum nach seinem Tod.*
> *Lass sie ruhn in deinem Schooss,*
> *erfüll' sie mit Freud' und Trost,*
> *bis der Leib kommt aus der Erde*
> *und mit ihr vereinigt werde.*

Terry, no. 107, presents his own translation.

The appearance of the chorale in the form as presented in the "371" is a condensation which we must regret very much, because the material that has been omitted removes from the chorale its tremendous festal quality. The original score shows *Violino I* and *Oboe I* on a separate staff supporting the soprano; similarly, *Violino II* and *Oboe II*, supporting the alto; *Viola* and *Taille*, supporting the tenor; and *Continuo*, supporting the bass. In addition to this instrumentation, *Trombe I, II, & III* and *Timpani* form an independent group, furnishing a quality to the chorale that is descriptive of the words, and expresses the atmosphere of the Resurrection.

299. Meinen Jesum lass ich nicht (n.s.)

300. Warum betrübst du dich, mein Herz (n.s.)

301. Ach, lieben Christen, seid getrost

This is known under the name "Wo Gott der Herr nicht bei uns hält", and closes Cantata 114, "Ach, lieben Christen, seid getrost". The stanza is the sixth of the hymn "Ach, lieben Christen, seid getrost".

> *Wir wachen oder schlafen ein,*
> *so sind wir doch des Herren;*

> *auf Christum wir getaufet sein,*
> *der kann dem Satan wehren.*
> *Durch Adam auf uns kömmt der Tod,*
> *Christus hilft uns aus aller Noth.*
> *Drum loben wir den Herren.*

Corno, *Oboi I & II*, and *Violino I* play with the soprano; *Violino II*, with the alto; *Viola*, with the tenor; and *Continuo*, with the bass.

Terry introduces a natural before the E in the bass and alto of the seventh measure. Schirmer B-R, I, p. 92, uses the translation by J. C. Jacobi. Terry, no. 399, presents his own translation.

302. Hilf, Gott, dass mir's gelinge (n.s.)

This is a duplicate of the harmonization under No. 199.

303. Herr Christ, der ein'ge Gott'ssohn

This harmonization brings to a close Cantata 96, "Herr Christ, der ein'ge Gottes-Sohn". The fifth stanza is used as the text:

> *Ertödt' uns durch dein' Güte,*
> *erweck' uns durch dein' Gnad';*
> *den alten Menschen kränke,*
> *dass der neu' leben mag*
> *wohl hier auf dieser Erden,*
> *den Sinn und all' Begehrden*
> *und G'danken hab'n zu dir.*

Corno, *Oboi I & II*, and *Violino I* play with the soprano; *Violino II*, with the alto; *Viola*, with the tenor; and *Continuo*, with the bass. Schirmer B-R, I, p. 82, uses an English translation by Miles Coverdale. Terry, no. 131, presents his own translation.

304. Auf meinen lieben Gott

This is the concluding number of Cantata 5, "Wo soll ich fliehen hin". The stanza is the eleventh one of the hymn "Wo soll ich fliehen hin".

> *Führ' auch mein Herz und Sinn*
> *durch deinen Geist dahin,*
> *dass ich mög' alles meiden,*
> *was mich und dich kann scheiden,*
> *und ich an deinem Leibe*
> *ein Gliedmass ewig bleibe.*

Terry, no. 28, uses his own English translation.

Violino I, Oboi I & II, and *Tromba da tirarsi* play with the soprano; *Violino II*, with the alto; *Viola*, with the tenor; and *Continuo*, with the bass.

305. Wie schön leuchtet der Morgenstern

Among the "371" exact duplicates of this harmonization are found under Nos. 86 and 195. For further details, see the notes on No. 86.

306. O Mensch, bewein' dein' Sünde gross (n.s.)

A duplicate of No. 201 in this edition.

307. Christus, der uns selig macht (n.s.)

This is a duplicate of No. 198.

308. Ach Gott, wie manches Herzeleid

Another duplicate, this time of No. 156, which is taken from Cantata 3, "Ach Gott wie manches Herzeleid".

309. Ein Lämmlein geht und trägt die Schuld (n.s.)

As No. 5 of the "371" this harmonization appeared under the name "An Wasserflüssen Babylon" and in the key of G. A few minor differences in the manner of notation are apparent; otherwise, the two chorales agree.

310. Mach's mit mir, Gott, nach deiner

This harmonization is found in Part II of the "St. John Passion", where it is used with a special stanza by C. H. Postel:

> *Durch dein Gefängniss, Gottes Sohn,*
> *ist uns die Freiheit kommen,*
> *dein Kerker is der Gnadenthron,*
> *die Freistatt aller Frommen;*
> *denn gingst du nicht die Knechtschaft ein,*
> *müsst' unsre Knechtschaft ewig sein.*

Schirmer B-R, I, p. 87, presents a translation by Dr. Charles N. Boyd. Terry, no. 242, presents his own translation.

Flauti traversi I & II, Oboi I & II, and *Violino I* play with the soprano; *Violino II*, with the

alto; *Viola*, with the tenor; and *Organo* and *Continuo*, with the bass.

311. Dank sei Gott in der Höhe (n.s.)

312. O Gott, du frommer Gott

This is the concluding number of the cantata "Ehre sei Gott in der Höhe", where it appears with the fourth stanza of the hymn "Ich freue mich in dir".

> *Wohlan! so will ich mich*
> *an dich, o Jesu, halten,*
> *und sollte gleich die Welt*
> *in tausend Stücken spalten.*
> *O Jesu, dir, nur dir,*
> *dir leb' ich ganz allein,*
> *auf dich, allein auf dich,*
> *mein Jesu, schlaf' ich ein.*

Terry, no. 284, offers his own translation.

No instruments are indicated for the chorale.

313. Allein Gott in der Höh' sei Ehr'

This harmonization concludes Cantata 112, "Der Herr ist mein getreuer Hirt", with the text from the hymn "Der Herr ist mein getreuer Hirt", stanza V:

> *Gutes und die Barmherzigkeit*
> *folgen mir nach im Leben,*
> *und ich werd' bleiben allezeit*
> *im Haus des Herren eben:*
> *auf Erd' in christlicher Gemein',*
> *und nach dem Tod da werd' ich sein*
> *bei Christo, meinem Herren.*

Schirmer B-R, II, no. 92, presents an English translation by Dr. Charles N. Boyd, along with the chorale harmonization in its original form. Terry, no. 16, publishes his own translation.

In the original form, two separate staves accommodate parts for *Corni I & II. Corno I* is almost a duplication of the soprano; *Corno II* is independent. In the present edition, the notes of these two horn parts are given in small notes wherever they offer material indispensable for an appreciation of the structure of the number. Each of the four voice-parts is supported by instruments: soprano by *Violino I* and *Oboe d'amore I*, alto by *Violino II* and *Oboe d'amore II* (which deviates from the voice part in places), tenor by *Viola*, and bass by *Continuo*.

An almost identical harmonization is presented farther on, as No. 353 of the "371", under the incorrect title "Der Herr is mein getreuer Hirt".

314. Das alte Jahr vergangen ist (n.s.)

315. O Gott, du frommer Gott (n.s.)

This melody is the lesser known melody under this name.

316. Christus, der ist mein Leben

This harmonization is so nearly like that of the opening chorus of Cantata 95, "Christus, der ist mein Leben", that one must decide that it was derived from that source. In the original score, fairly long orchestral interludes are occupied with a rather lively orchestration which continues during the singing of the chorale by the chorus. Several minor changes in the reproduction of the passing notes have also been made for the present condensation. The student is advised to refer to the full score of the cantata.

317. Herr, wie du willst, so schick's mit mir

This chorale closes Cantata 156, "Ich steh' mit einem Fuss im Grabe". It makes use of the first stanza:

> *Herr, wie du will't, so schick's mit mir*
> *im Leben und im Sterben;*
> *allein zu dir steht mein Begehr,*
> *Herr, lass mich nicht verderben!*
> *Erhalt' mich nur in deiner Huld,*
> *sonst, wie du will't, gieb mir Geduld;*
> *dein Will' der ist der beste.*

Schirmer B-R, I, p. 99, uses a translation by Dr. Emanuel Cronenwett. Terry, no. 153, provides his own translation.

Oboe and *Violino I* play with the soprano; *Violino II*, with the alto; *Viola*, with the tenor; and *Continuo*, with the bass.

318. Herr, wie du willst, so schick's mit mir (n.s.)

This is a duplicate of No. 144, which appears under the name of "Wer in den Schutz des Höchsten".

319. Sanctus, Sanctus, Dominus Deus Sabaoth (n.s.)

This is the same harmonization as was seen under the name "Heilig, heilig" in No. 235.

320. Gott sei uns gnädig und barmherzig (n.s.)

This is better known as "Meine Seele erhebt den Herren" and is the tune commonly called the German Magnificat, with the specific name *Tonus peregrinus*.

321. Wir Christenleut'

This harmonization occupies a position approximately in the middle of Cantata 40, "Dazu ist erschienen der Sohn Gottes". The text is the third stanza of the hymn.

> *Die Sünd' macht Leid,*
> *die Sünd' macht Leid;*
> *Christus bringt Freud',*
> *weil er zu Trost in diese Welt gekommen.*
>
> *Mit uns ist Gott*
> *nun in der Noth:*
> *wer ist, der uns als Christen kann verdammen?*

Schirmer B-R, I, p. 109, uses a translation by Catherine Winkworth. Terry, no. 396, employs his own translation.

Corno I, Oboe I, and *Violino I* play with the soprano; *Oboe II* and *Violino II*, with the alto; *Viola*, with the tenor; and *Continuo*, with the bass.

322. Wenn mein Stündlein vorhanden ist (n.s.)

323. Wie schön leuchtet der Morgenstern

The harmonization which closes Cantata 172, "Erschallet, ihr Lieder", is the source of this number, but it has been changed here in many respects. The stanza used is the fourth:

> *Von Gott kommt mir ein Freudenschein,*
> *wenn du mit deinen Äugelein*
> *mich freundlich thust anblicken.*
> *O Herr Jesu, mein trautes Gut,*
> *dein Wort, dein Geist, dein Leib und Blut*
> *mich innerlich erquicken.*
> *Nimm mich*

freundlich
in dein' Arme,
dass ich warme
werd' von Gnaden:
Auf dein Wort komm' ich geladen.

Terry, no. 394, presents his own translation.

An independent obbligato for *Violino I* plays above the vocal parts in a florid manner. *Violino II*, *Viola I*, *Viola II*, and *Continuo* with *Fagotto* are placed upon separate staves but agree with the soprano, alto, tenor and bass respectively.

324. Jesu, meine Freude

In this form the chorale is the closing number of Cantata 81, "Jesus schläft, was soll ich hoffen?". The stanza is the second of the hymn.

Unter deinen Schirmen
bin ich vor den Stürmen
aller Feinde frei.
Lass den Satan wittern,
lass den Feind erbittern,
mir steht Jesus bei.
Ob es jetzt gleich kracht und blitzt,
obgleich Sünd' und Hölle schrecken:
Jesus will mich decken.

Terry, no. 212, offers his own translation.
Oboi d'amore I & II and *Violino I* play with the soprano; *Violino II*, with the alto; *Viola*, with the tenor; and *Continuo*, with the bass.

325. Mit Fried' und Freud' ich fahr' dahin

This harmonization concludes Cantata 83, "Erfreute Zeit im neuen Bunde", using the fourth stanza of the hymn.

Er ist das Heil und selig Licht
für die Heiden,
zu erleuchten, die dich kennen nicht,
und zu weiden.
Er ist dein's Volks Israel
der Preis, Ehr', Freud' und Wonne.

Schirmer B-R, I, p. 101, uses the English translation by Catherine Winkworth; Terry, no. 258, offers his own translation.
Oboe I, *Corno I*, and *Violino I* play with the soprano; *Oboe II* and *Violino II*, with the alto; *Viola*, with the tenor; and *Continuo*, with the bass.

326. Allein Gott in der Höh' sei Ehr'

The harmonization of this chorale is duplicated in No. 125, with two exceptions: the key has been changed to G major and the next-to-last measure differs both in the melody and the harmonization. Since, however, the coincidence is so great, it appears that the writer of the manuscript, who evidently transposed the chorale, also undertook to change the measure in question.

The chorale closes Cantata 104, "Du Hirte Israel, höre", where it appears with the first stanza of "Der Herr ist mein getreuer Hirt".

Der Herr ist mein getreuer Hirt,
dem ich mich ganz vertraue,
zur Weid' er mich, sein Schäflein, führt,
auf schöner, grüner Aue;
zum frischen Wasser leit't er mich,
mein' Seel' zu laben kräftiglich
durch's sel'ge Wort der Gnaden.

Terry, no. 17, presents his own translation.
Oboe I and *Violino I* play with the soprano; *Oboe II* and *Violino II*, with the alto; *Taille* and *Viola*, with the tenor; and *Continuo*, with the bass. In the eighth and ninth measures, the *Taille* differs slightly from the tenor, extra notes being used to fill out the harmony.

327. Jesu, nun sei gepreiset

This chorale brings Cantata 190, "Singet dem Herrn ein neues Lied", to a triumphant close. Much of the chorale has been omitted in this arrangement. In the original score *Oboi I, II, & III*, *Violini I & II*, *Viola*, and *Continuo* have been given separate staves. *Oboe I* and *Violino I* duplicate the soprano; *Viola* and *Continuo* duplicate the tenor and bass, respectively. More or less independent are the parts assigned to *Oboi II & III* and *Violino II*. In addition to this orchestration, Bach employed three trumpets and the kettledrums. Nine times, including the repeats, he has these instruments enter in four-part fanfare groups, each two measures in length. This creates a festal atmosphere for the chorale which is totally lacking in the present condensation

The following stanza is used.

Lass uns das Jahr vollbringen
zu Lob dem Namen dein,
dass wir demselben singen
in der Christengemein;
wollst uns das Leben fristen
durch dein' allmächtig' Hand,
erhalt' dein' liebe Christen
und unser Vaterland.
Dein'n Segen zu uns wende,
gieb Fried' an allem Ende;
gieb unverfälscht im Lande
dein seligmachend Wort.
Die Heuchler mach' zu Schande
hier und an allem Ort,
die Heuchler mach' zu Schande
hier und an allem Ort.

Terry does not print this harmonization, probably because it belongs to the more complex type, but he presents an English translation for the stanza under a different harmonization in his number 216.

328. Liebster Jesu, wir sind hier (n.s.)

With one very slight change in the tenor of the last measure but one, this harmonization is a repetition of the one listed under No. 131.

329. Sei Lob und Ehr' dem höchsten Gut

This is one of the three wedding chorales. It was designed to be sung after the ceremony and before the blessing. The melody is known under the name "Es ist das Heil uns kommen her". The name given for it in this number of the "371" is derived from the stanza used:

Sei Lob und Ehr' dem höchsten Gut,
dem Vater aller Güte,
dem Gott, der alle Wunder thut,
dem Gott, der mein Gemüthe
mit seinem reichen Trost erfüllt,
dem Gott, der allen Jammer stillt:
gebt unserm Gott die Ehre!

Schirmer, B-R, book II, nos. 114-116, presents the three Wedding Chorales in their original form. Terry, no. 92, offers his own translation.

The instruments used with these three wedding chorales are identical. Two *obbligati* for *Corno I* and *Corno II* are presented upon separate staves. *Corno I* agrees with the soprano; *Corno II* is usually an independent part. In addition,

Oboe I and *Violino I* play with the soprano; *Oboe d'amore* and *Violino II*, with the alto; *Viola*, with the tenor; and *Organo* and *Continuo*, with the bass.

330. Nun danket alle Gott

What has been said in the remarks under No. 329 applies also to this chorale, which is the third of the group of Wedding Chorales and was designed to be sung after the blessing was pronounced. The relation of the instrum its also remains the same as in the preceding chorale. The stanza is the first:

Nun danket alle Gott
mit Herzen, Mund und Händen,
der grosse Dinge thut
an uns und allen Enden;
der uns von Mutterleib
und Kindesbeinen an
unzählig viel zu gut,
und noch jetzund, gethan.

Terry, no. 265, and Schirmer B-R, book II, no. 116, use the translation by Catherine Winkworth.

331. Wo soll ich fliehen hin

This harmonization concludes Cantata 136, "Erforsche mich, Gott, und erfahre mein Herz". The melody is usually known under the name "Auf meinen lieben Gott". The ninth stanza is used:

Dein Blut, der edle Saft,
hat solche Stärk' und Kraft,
dass auch die Tröpflein kleine
die ganze Welt kann reine,
ja, gar aus Teufels Rachen
frei, los und ledig machen.

Terry, no. 30, offers his own English translation.

Corno and *Oboi I & II* play with the soprano; *Violino II*, with the alto; *Viola*, with the tenor; and *Continuo*, with the bass. Over the whole the *Violino I* plays a free and florid obbligato.

332. Von Gott will ich nicht lassen (n.s.)

333. Es woll' uns Gott genädig sein

This harmonization brings to a triumphant conclusion Cantata 69, "Lobe den Herrn, meine Seele". The stanza used is the third:

Es danke, Gott, und lobe dich
das Volk in guten Thaten.
Das Land bringt Frucht und bessert sich,
dein Wort ist wohl gerathen.
Uns segne Vater und der Sohn,
uns segne Gott, der heil'ge Geist,
dem alle Welt die Ehre thu',
vor ihm sich fürchte allermeist,
und sprecht von Herzen: Amen!

In the present edition of the "371" the parts for *Trombe I, II, & III* have been given in small notes. The *Timpani* part, which also adds much to the festal character of the number, has been omitted. Other instruments used in the chorale and agreeing in general with the voices are *Oboi I, II, & III*, Strings, *Fagotto*, and *Continuo*. The student is referred to Schirmer B-R, book II, no. 94, where the complete original form of the chorale is given together with a translation by the author of these notes.

334. Für deinen Thron tret' ich hiermit
(n.s.)

This chorale should bear the name "Herr Gott, dich loben alle wir".

335. Es ist das Heil uns kommen her

This chorale is found as the final number of Cantata 155, "Mein Gott, wie lang', ach lange". The twelfth stanza is used as the text:

Ob sich's anliess', als wollt' er nicht,
lass dich es nicht erschrecken,
denn wo er ist am besten mit,
da will er's nicht entdecken;
sein Wort lass dir gewisser sein,
und ob dein Herz spräch' lauter Nein,
so lass doch dir nicht grauen.

Schirmer B-R, I, p. 96, uses a translation by J. C. Jacobi. Terry, no. 91, presents his own translation.
Violino I, Violino II, Viola, and *Continuo* duplicate the four voice parts.

336. Wo Gott der Herr nicht bei uns hält
(n.s.)

337. O Gott, du frommer Gott

In a much more elaborate and complete form, this harmonization closes Cantata 24, "Ein

ungefärbt Gemüthe". The first stanza is used as the text:

O Gott, du frommer Gott,
du Brunnquell aller Gaben,
ohn' den nichts ist, was ist,
von dem wir Alles haben:
gesunden Leib gieb mir,
und dass in solchem Leib'
ein' unverletzte Seel'
und rein Gewissen bleib',
und rein Gewissen bleib'!

Terry, no. 289, presents the translation by Catherine Winkworth.

It has not proved feasible to present in this edition the complete form of this very elaborate chorale. Accordingly, no changes have been made in the considerably reduced version of it that has traditionally appeared among the "371". This reduced version takes into consideration only the voice parts, and omits the instrumental interludes. In so doing, it shifts the beginning of at least three verse lines from the fourth beat to the second beat or from the second to the fourth. Moreover, two full measures at the end of the complete chorale, where the last verse line was repeated, do not appear in this version. The instrumental interludes form a brilliant independent part played by *Clarino, Oboi I & II*, Strings, and *Continuo*. Interested students should consult the full score as published in the Bachgesellschaft Edition.

338. Jesus, meine Zuversicht

This is one of those unusual instances where a simply harmonized chorale opens a cantata—in this case, Cantata 145, "So du mit deinem Munde bekennest Jessum". The stanza used is the first one:

Auf, mein Herz! Des Herren Tag
hat die Nacht der Furcht vertrieben:
Christus, der im Grabe lag,
ist im Tode nicht geblieben.
Nunmehr bin ich recht getröst't,
Jesus hat die Welt erlöst.

Schirmer B-R, I, p. 86, offers a translation by Dr. Charles N. Boyd. Terry, no. 222, employs his own translation.

No special instruments are designated for the chorale. No doubt the instruments used for the cantata were employed. They are: *Tromba, Flauto traverso, Oboi d'amore I & II*, Strings, and *Continuo*.

339. Wer nur den lieben Gott lässt walten

This brings to a close Cantata 179, "Siehe zu, dass deine Gottesfurcht nicht Heuchelei sei". The stanza is the first one of the hymn "Ich armer Mensch, ich armer Sünder".

> *Ich armer Mensch, ich armer Sünder*
> *steh' hier vor Gottes Angesicht.*
> *Ach Gott, ach Gott, verfahr' gelinder*
> *und geh' nicht mit mir in's Gericht.*
> *Erbarme dich, erbarme dich,*
> *Gott mein Erbarmer, über mich!*

Terry, no. 378, presents his own translation.

The only instrumental indications are: *Oboi I & II* with the soprano and *Continuo* with the bass. No doubt the Strings were also used in their customary way.

340. Befiehl du deine Wege (n.s.)

This melody is correctly named. The other harmonizations appearing under this name—Nos. 270, 286, and 367—are wrongly named, and should be called "Herzlich tut mich verlangen".

341. Ich dank' dir, lieber Herre

This closes Cantata 37, "Wer da glaubet und getauft wird". The stanza is the fourth:

> *Den Glauben mir verleihe*
> *an dein'n Sohn, Jesum Christ,*
> *mein' Sünd' mir auch verzeihe*
> *allhier, zu dieser Frist.*
> *Du wirst mir's nicht versagen,*
> *was du verheissen hast,*
> *dass er mein' Sünd' thu' tragen*
> *und lös' mich von der Last.*

Schirmer B-R, I, p. 113, offers an original translation by Dr. Charles N. Boyd. Terry, no. 182, presents his own translation.

Oboe d'amore I and *Violino I* play with the soprano; *Oboe d'amore II* and *Violino II*, with the alto; *Viola*, with the tenor; and *Continuo*, with the bass.

342. Lobt Gott, ihr Christen, allzugleich (n.s.)

343. Nun lieget alles unter dir

This melody should be called "Ermuntre dich, mein schwacher Geist". It is found in about the middle portion of Cantata 11, "Lobet Gott in seinen Reichen". The stanza is the fourth:

> *Nun lieget alles unter dir,*
> *dich selbst nur ausgenommen;*
> *die Engel müssen für und für*
> *dir aufzuwarten kommen.*
> *Die Fürsten stehn auch auf der Bahn,*
> *und sind dir willig unterthan;*
> *Luft, Wasser, Feu'r und Erden*
> *muss dir zu Dienste werden.*

Terry, no. 83, gives his own translation.

Flauti traversi I & II (in 8va), *Oboe I*, and *Violino I* play with the soprano; *Oboe II* and *Violino II*, with the alto; *Viola*, with the tenor; and *Continuo*, with the bass.

344. Vom Himmel hoch, da komm' ich her

This is another one of those chorales which, in the "371", have suffered greatly because of contraction. In its original form it brings to a close Part II of the "Christmas Oratorio" with the words of the second stanza of the hymn "Wir singen dir, Immanuel".

> *Wir singen dir in deinem Heer*
> *aus aller Kraft: Lob, Preis und Ehr',*
> *dass du, o lang gewünschter Gast,*
> *dich nunmehr eingestellet hast.*

Terry, no. 336, offers his own translation.

The instrumental interludes have been omitted. These were each two measures in length and in the style of the pastorale symphony. The second and the fourth verse-lines originally began on the second beat; with the omission of the interludes, they have been shifted to the fourth beat. The Strings duplicate the voice parts, while *Flauti traversi I & II*, *Oboi d'amore I & II*, and *Oboi da caccia I & II* form an individual pastorale group of contrasting material which is used to alternate with the voice parts. In this edition of the "371", the *Continuo* for this number has been written an octave lower than in the score. In its form as here used it is only the skeleton of the real chorale; the original should be consulted if a serious study of this harmonization is undertaken.

345. O Haupt voll Blut und Wunden

This chorale, which is known under the name "Herzlich thut much verlangen", is placed about the middle of Part I of the "Christmas Oratorio", to the first stanza of the hymn "Wie soll ich dich empfangen".

> *Wie soll ich dich empfangen,*
> *und wie begegn' ich dir?*
> *o aller Welt Verlangen,*
> *o meiner Seelen Zier!*
> *O Jesu, Jesu! setze*
> *mir selbst die Fackel bei,*
> *damit, was dich ergötze,*
> *mir kund und wissend sei.*

Terry, no. 162, offers the translation by Catherine Winkworth.
Flauto traverso (*in 8ᵛᵃ*), *Oboi I & II*, and *Violino I* play with the soprano; *Violino II*, with the alto; *Viola*, with the tenor; and *Fagotto, Organo,* and *Continuo*, with the bass.

346. Meines Lebens letzte Zeit (n.s.)

This is a realization of the melody and figured bass that appears as number 63 in the Schemelli group. For students who are studying how to harmonize figured basses, a comparison should prove most valuable.

347. Was Gott tut, das ist wohlgetan

This is the first of a series of three Wedding Chorales which Bach wrote for a wedding service. This one was to be sung before the wedding. It uses the first stanza of the hymn.

> *Was Gott thut, das ist wohlgethan,*
> *es bleibt gerecht sein Wille;*
> *wie er fängt meine Sachen an,*
> *will ich ihm halten stille.*
> *Er ist mein Gott,*
> *der in der Noth*
> *mich wohl weiss zu erhalten;*
> *drum lass ich ihn nur walten.*

Schirmer B-R, book II, no. 114, presents a translation by E. Cronenwett, and in nos. 114-116 presents the three Wedding Chorales in their original form. Terry, no. 355, presents his own translation.

As in the other wedding chorales, *Oboe I* and *Violino I* play with the soprano; *Oboe d'amore* and *Violino II*, with the alto; *Viola*, with the tenor; and *Organo* and *Continuo*, with the bass. *Corno I* plays with the soprano, but is given a separate staff for its part. *Corno II* plays an independent obbligato part, which has been included in small notes in the present edition of the "371", along with such of the *Corno I* notes as are indispensable to this version. The other two wedding chorales are found under No. 329 and 330.

348. Meinen Jesum lass ich nicht

This is a condensation of the chorale that closes Cantata 70, "Wachet, betet, seid bereit allezeit". The stanza used is the fifth:

> *Nicht nach Welt, nach Himmel nicht*
> *meine Seele wünscht und sehnet,*
> *Jesum wünsch' ich und sein Licht,*
> *der mich hat mit Gott versöhnet,*
> *der mich frei macht vom Gericht,*
> *meinen Jesum lass' ich nicht.*

Schirmer B-R, book II, no. 108, presents the chorale in its complete form, together with an original translation by the author of these notes. Terry, no. 249, presents his own translation.

The original chorale has a *Tromba* and an *Oboe* part (on separate staves) which agree with the soprano, and a *Fagotto* and *Continuo* which agree with the bass. In addition, three independent florid parts for *Violino I*, *Violino II*, and *Viola* add greatly to the rich effect of the harmonization. The omission of the String parts in the present reduction is a very great loss.

349. Ich hab' in Gottes Herz und Sinn

This is an exact duplication of the harmonization of No. 120, "Was mein Gott will, das g'scheh allezeit". It closes Cantata 103, "Ihr werdet weinen und heulen".

350. Jesu, meiner Seelen Wonne (n.s.)

The name of this chorale is "Werde munter, mein Gemüthe".

351. Wenn mein Stündlein vorhanden ist (n.s.)

352. Es woll' uns Gott genädig sein (n.s.)

353. Der Herr ist mein getreuer Hirt

This number is practically a duplicate of No. 313. Information about its original form is given in the note under that number.

354. Sei Lob und Ehr' dem höchsten Gut

This is a duplicate of No. 248 in this collection. For its origin please refer to that number.

355. Nun ruhen alle Wälder

This harmonization closes Cantata 44, "Sie werden euch in den Bann thun". The stanza used is the fifteenth of the hymn "In allen meinen Thaten".

So sei nun, Seele, deine,
und traue dem alleine,
der dich erschaffen hat.
Es gehe, wie es gehe:
dein Vater in der Höhe,
der weiss zu allen Sachen Rath.

Terry presents his own translation in his number 306.
Oboe I and *Violino I* play with the soprano; *Oboe II* and *Violino II*, with the alto; *Viola*, with the tenor; and *Fagotto* and *Continuo*, with the bass.

356. Jesu, meine Freude (n.s.)

357. Warum sollt' ich mich denn grämen (n.s.)

358. Meine Seel' erhebt den Herren

This melody is known as the German Magnificat. It is of Pre-Reformation origin, and was known as the *Tonus peregrinus*. It is found as the concluding number of Cantata 10, "Meine Seel' erhebt den Herren".

Lob und Preis sei Gott dem Vater and dem Sohn
und dem heiligen Geiste, wie es war im An-
fang jetzt und immerdar and von Ewigkeit zu
Ewigkeit, Amen.

Violino I, Oboi I & II, and *Tromba* play with the soprano; *Violino II*, with the alto; *Viola*, with the tenor; and *Continuo*, with the bass.
A shorter version is found in this edition under No. 130.

359. Allein zu dir, Herr Jesu Christ (n.s.)

360. Wir Christenleut'

This brings to a close Part III of the Christmas Oratorio" with the text of the fourth stanza:

Seid froh, dieweil,
seid froh, dieweil
dass euer Heil
ist hie ein Gott und auch ein Mensch geboren,
der welcher ist
der Herr und Christ
in Davids Stadt, von Vielen auserkoren.

Terry, no. 395, presents his own English translation.
Flauti traversi I & II (in 8ᵛᵃ), Oboi I & II, and *Violino I* play with the soprano; *Violino II*, with the alto; *Viola*, with the tenor; and *Organo* and *Continuo*, with the bass.

361. Du Lebensfürst, Herr Jesu Christ

This melody is usually known under the name "Ermuntre dich, mein schwacher Geist". It is found in Part II of the "Christmas Oratorio". A duplication of this harmonization may be found under No. 9 of this edition. For details concerning this chorale, please refer to the description under No. 9 of this book.

362. Es ist gewisslich an der Zeit

This is more often known under the name "Nun freut euch, lieben Christen g'mein". It occupies a position in about the middle of the "Christmas Oratorio", Part VI. The stanza used is the following:

Ich steh' an deiner Krippen hier,
o Jesulein, mein Leben,
ich komme, bring' und schenke dir,

was du mir hast gegeben.
Nimm hin, es ist mein Geist und Sinn,
Herz, Seel' und Muth, nimm Alles hin,
und lass dir's wohl gefallen!

Schirmer B-R, I, p. 123, offers a translation by the author of these notes. Terry, no. 269, presents his own translation.

Oboi I & II and *Violino I* play with the soprano; *Violino II*, with the alto; *Viola*, with the tenor; and *Organo* and *Continuo*, with the bass. The instrumental bass, consisting of *Continuo* and *Organo*, has a part that shows considerable elaboration over the vocal bass.

363. O Welt, sieh hier dein Leben (n.s.)

This is more familiar under the name "O Welt, ich muss dich lassen". No source is known for this chorale, but it is so similar to No. 63 of this set, which was derived from the "St. John Passion", that the latter may have been its origin. Please refer to the notes for No. 63.

364. Von Gott will ich nicht lassen (n.s.)

365. Jesu, meiner Seelen Wonne (n.s.)

This chorale is better known under the name "Werde munter, mein Gemüthe". This form of the chorale has a great similarity to No. 233, which was taken from Cantata 154, "Mein liebster Jesus ist verloren". A comparison of the two harmonizations presents much of interest to the student.

366. O Welt, sieh hier dein Leben (n.s.)

This chorale is better known as "O Welt, ich muss dich lassen".

367. Befiehl du deine Wege (n.s.)

The more usual name for this chorale is "Herzlich thut mich verlangen". It has been harmonized many times by Bach.

368. Hilf, Herr Jesu, lass gelingen

There are two chorale melodies known under this title. The other one may be found as No. 155.

This harmonization is an exact reproduction of the notes of the voice parts of an extended harmonization which brings to a close Part IV of the "Christmas Oratorio". Bach's complete version represents immeasurably more than the form of the present reduction. In fact, the vocal parts are only a kernel around which the instrumental parts play a wonderful and colorful obbligato. Between each verse line of the vocal chorale are four measures of rests for the voices during which time the instruments carry on the continuity of the chorale.

Corno I, Corno II, Oboe I, Oboe II, Strings, and *Organo e Continuo* are all assigned independent parts. It is impossible to judge the effect and beauty of the whole chorale from the vocal parts alone as presented in the "371".

The stanza used is the fifteenth:

Jesus richte mein Beginnen,
Jesus bleibe stets bei mir;
Jesus zäume mir die Sinnen,
Jesus sei nur mein' Begier.
Jesus sei mir in Gedanken,
Jesu, lasse mich nicht wanken!

Schirmer B-R, book II, no. 97, presents the original form with a translation by Catherine Winkworth. Terry, no. 178, offers his own translation.

369. Jesu, der du meine Seele (n.s.)

370. Kommt her zu mir, spricht Gottes Sohn

This harmonization brings to a close Cantata 74, "Wer mich liebet, der wird mein Wort halten". The stanza is the second one of the hymn "Gott, Vater, sende deinen Geist".

Kein Menschenkind hier auf der Erd'
ist dieser edlen Gabe werth,
bei uns ist kein Verdienen;
hier gilt gar nichts als Lieb' und Gnad',
die Christus uns verdienet hat
mit Büssen und Versühnen.

Schirmer B-R, I, p. 101, offers a translation by Dr. Charles N. Boyd. Terry, no. 229, offers his own translation.

Tromba I, *Oboe I*, and *Violino I* play with the soprano; *Oboe II* and *Violino II*, with the alto; *Oboe da caccia* and *Viola*, with the tenor; and *Continuo*, with the bass.

371. Christ lag in Todesbanden (n.s.)

The source of this comparatively complex harmonization has been lost. Other harmonizations of this same melody are found among the "371", as Nos. 15, 184, and 261. The student can find no more profitable study in harmony than to compare the various harmonizations of the same melodies which are found in this edition.

THE 69 CHORALE MELODIES
WITH FIGURED BASS

ALTHOUGH the 69 melodies with figured bass were published in Schemelli's *Gesangbuch* as early as 1736 and republished by C. F. Becker in 1832 as an addendum to the 371 Chorales, very little was known about them except by students of harmony and connoisseurs of figured basses.

It was almost prophetic of the activities of the Neue Bachgesellschaft, which was formed at the dissolution of the older Bachgesellschaft, that its first project was concerned with these very melodies. The Neue Bachgesellschaft selected as its objective the development of the use of J. S. Bach's compositions for practical purposes. Since the publication by the Neue Bachgesellschaft of the volume called *Lieder und Arien für eine Singstimme und Pianoforte* these melodies have become widely known under the name *Geistliche Lieder* ("spiritual songs"). They have entered freely into the church and concert repertory of our best singers.

A short description of the main publications covering these works follows. In the tabulation following the index, the numbers under which they may be found in each edition are designated.

1. Johann Sebastian Bach, *Zwanzig Geistliche Lieder ausgearbeitet von* Robert Franz.

This work was published by F. E. C. Leuckart, Leipzig. It is undated but was probably issued in the 1880's. This was the first publication of a group of these songs for practical purposes. It will be identified in the index by the words **Franz Edition.**

2. *Twenty Sacred Songs, composed by Johann Sebastian Bach.*

This is an English translation of the above. The translations are by the Rev. Dr. Troutbeck and the publisher is Novello and Company, Limited, London. It will appear under the name **Novello.**

3. Joh. Seb. Bach, *Lieder und Arien*

Publication of the Neue Bachgesellschaft. The set appeared in 1901 under the editorship of Ernst Naumann. It consists of 75 compositions and an addendum of *"Drei Arien"* from the Notebook for Anna Magdalena Bach. Following the harmonies designated by the figured basses, Naumann has arranged these melodies for solo voice and piano or organ.

This edition has since been transferred to the regular catalogue of Breitkopf and Härtel, and five additional arias from the manuscript of Johann Ludwig Krebs have been added to the book, making the addendum eight arias instead of three. An edition for low voice under the editorship of Martin is also published by Breit-

kopf and Härtel. For convenience this edition will be designated **Neue Bachgesellschaft** in the index.

4. Johann Sebastian Bach, *Lieder und Arien für vierstimmigen gemischten Chor.*

This is the second publication of the Neue Bachgesellschaft, and is edited and arranged by Franz Wüllner. It contains the first 75 numbers of the preceding publication and is arranged for soprano, alto, tenor, and bass, using the C clefs. This will be designated in the index as **Wüllner.**

5. *J. S. Bach's Gesänge zu Schemelli's Musicalischem Gesangbuch, 1736.* This is a publication of the Bärenreiter-Verlag in Kassel. The editor is the famous German Bach authority and musicologist, Max Seiffert. The date of the preface is 1924. It contains only the 69 melodies of the present set, which are placed in various groups, such as morning songs, evening songs, *etc.*, just as they were in the original Schemelli *Gesangbuch.* The arrangement is for solo voice and piano or organ accompaniment. It will be designated in the index as **Seiffert.**

6. Johann Sebastian Bach, *Geistliche Lieder aus Schemelli's Gesangbuch und dem Notenbuch der Anna Magdalena Bach ausgewählt.*

This is a selection of fifteen of this type arranged and edited by Ludwig Landshoff for solo voice and pipe organ with pedal. It will be indicated in the index as **Landshoff.**

7. Johann Sebastian Bach, *32 Hengellistä laulua.*

This is published by Werner Söderström Osakeyhtiö, Porvoo. It is edited by John Sundberg for solo voice and piano. All of the numbers are from the group of 69 except number 6, which is the chorale taken from Cantata 40, "Dazu ist erschienen", and number 7, which is from the Notebook for Anna Magdalena Bach. There is a preface by Alekei Lehtonen, Helsingfors, dated May, 1925. This publication shows how extended has been the growth of appreciation for these simple songs. This edition will be indicated in the index under the name **Sundberg.**

8. Bach, *25 Geistliche Lieder*, edited by Herman Roth, published by C. F. Peters, Leipzig, indicated below as **Peters.**

No more advantageous study may be undertaken by the student than to make a comparison of the 69 melodies with figured basses and their realization in these eight groups or partial groups. It offers to the student of harmony a practical and living example of harmony applied to its use in composition.

Attention has been called in the notes to the 371 chorales, concerning eight of these melodies to which Bach himself left realizations, namely, Nos. 18, 22, 26, 36, 53, 55, 63, and 65. They are found in the "371" as Nos. 220, 172, 206, 234, 244, 193, 346, and 213 respectively.

INDEX OF THE 69 CHORALE MELODIES
ACCORDING TO NUMBER (in this and other editions)

TITLES	69 Chorale Melodies	Franz Edition	Novello	Neue Bach-gesellschaft	Wüllner	Seiffert	Landshoff	Sundberg	Peters
Ach, dass nicht die letzte Stunde........	56	10	10	1	1	56	13		21
Auf, auf! die rechte Zeit ist hier	11			2	2	11			1
Auf, auf! mein Herz, mit Freuden........	27	7	7	3	3	27		18	
Beglückter Stand getreuer...............	39			4	4	39			
Beschränkt, ihr Weisen dieser...........	47			5	5	47			11
Brich entzwei, mein armes..............	24			6	6	24	12	14	5
Brunnquell aller Güter..................	29			7	7	29			
Der lieben Sonnen Licht................	2			8	8	2			
Der Tag ist hin, die Sonne gehet........	3			9	9	3		32	
Der Tag mit seinem Lichte..............	4			10	10	4		31	
Dich bet' ich an, mein höchster..........	31			11	11	31			19
Die bittre Leidenszeit beginnet..........	17	5	5	12	12	17		13	
Die goldne Sonne, voll Freud'..........	1			13	13	1		21	
Dir, dir, Jehovah, will ich..............	32			14	14	32		27	18
Eins ist not! ach Herr, dies.............	7			15	15	7			16
Ermuntre dich, mein schwacher..........	12			16	16	12			
Erwürgtes Lamm, das die..............	43	17	17	17	17	43		19	
Es glänzet der Christen.................	40			18	18	40			
Es ist nun aus mit meinem..............	57			19	19	57			
Es ist vollbracht! vergiss ja.............	25	12	12	20	20	25		15	
Es kostet viel, ein Christ zu............	38			21	21	38			
Gieb dich zufrieden und sei.............	45	16	16	24	24	45		25	
Gott lebet noch, Seele was..............	37			25	25	37		8	
Gott, wie gross ist deine Güte...........	30			26	26	30			9
Herr, nicht schicke deine Rache........	5			27	27	5			
Ich bin ja, Herr, in deiner.............	58			28	28	58			

TITLES	69 Chorale Melodies	Franz Edition	Novello	Neue Bach-gesellschaft	Wüllner	Seiffert	Landshoff	Sundberg	Peters
Ich freue mich in dir, und..............	13			29	29	13		5	
Ich halte treulich still und liebe..........	46			30	30	46	6		10
Ich lass' dich nicht, du musst	51			31	31	51			13
Ich liebe Jesum alle Stund'..............	52			32	32	52		10	12
Ich steh' an deiner Krippen.............	14			33	33	14		3	2
Ihr Gestirn', ihr hohlen Lüfte...........	15			40	40	15		26	
Jesu, deine Liebeswunden..............	10			35	35	10			8
Jesus ist das schönste Licht.............	33			38	38	33			
Jesu, Jesu, du bist mein................	53			34	34	53		9	14
Jesu, meines Glaubens Zier.............	8			36	36	8			
Jesu, meines Herzens Freud'............	48			37	37	48			
Jesus, unser Trost und Leben	28	3	3	39	39	28			
Kein Stündlein geht dahin..............	60			41	41	60			
Komm, süsser Tod, komm sel'ge........	59	11	11	42	42	59	10	28	22
Kommt, Seelen, dieser Tag.............	67	2	2	43	43	67	8	20	7
Kommt, wieder aus der finstern Gruft....	68	15	15	44	44	68	4	16	6
Lasset uns mit Jesu ziehen	18			45	45	18			
Liebes Herz, bedenke doch.............	34			46	46	34			
Liebster Gott, wann werd' ich..........	61			47	47	61			
Liebster Herr Jesu! wo bleibest.........	62	1	1	48	48	62		29	15
Liebster Immanuel, Herzog.............	54			49	49	54		2	
Meines Lebens letzte Zeit..............	63			52	52	63			23
Mein Jesu, dem die Seraphinen.........	9			50	50	9		22	
Mein Jesu! was für Seelenweh	19	4	4	51	51	19	5	11	4
Nicht so traurig, nicht.................	41	6	6	53	53	41			
Nur mein Jesus ist mein Leben.........	49			54	54	49			
O du Liebe meiner Liebe...............	20			55	55	20			
O finstre Nacht......................	64	20	20	57	57	64		24	25
O Jesulein süss, o Jesulein.............	16	8	8	58	58	16	15	4	
O liebe Seele, zieh die Sinnen..........	42			59	59	42		1	17
O wie selig seid ihr doch, ihr	65			60	60	65			
Seelen-Bräutigam, Jesu................	35			62	62	35			
Seelenweide, meine Freude.............	50			63	63	50			
Sei gegrüsset, Jesu gütig...............	22			65	65	22			
Selig, wer an Jesum denkt	21	9	9	64	64	21	11	12	3
So gehst du nun, mein Jesu.............	23	13	13	66	66	23			
So giebst du nun, mein Jesu............	26			67	67	26			
So wünsch ich mir zu guter............	66	19	19	68	68	66		30	24
Steh ich bei meinem Gott..............	69			69	69	69			
Vergiss mein nicht, vergiss mein nicht....	44	14	14	71	71	44	14	23	20
Vergiss mein nicht, dass ich dein nicht....	36			70	70	36			
Was bist du doch, o Seele..............	55			73	73	55			
Wo ist mein Schäflein, das ich	6	18	18	75	75	6		17	